T0013403

"Many good Christians assume the[...] But Skye Jethani calls us to think a[...] vision of heaven have come from cultural assumptions [...]. With his characteristic clarity and signature illustrations, Skye helps us rediscover what heaven meant to Jesus. More than that, he invites us to recognize that heaven is not our future destination but rather God's present location—the place where he dwells and rules—and thus represents the shape of our mission on earth. This book offers a life-altering paradigm shift, because how we think about heaven affects how we live on earth."

—**Glenn Packiam**, lead pastor, Rockharbor Church; author of *The Resilient Pastor* and *The Intentional Year*

"There are few topics more misunderstood in the American church than heaven. *What If Jesus Was Serious about Heaven?* addresses our confusion with thoughtful provocations, insightful corrections, and solid biblical teaching. This is a resource that doesn't just fix bad theology; it also orients believers in Christ toward the beautiful picture of cosmic redemption actually found in Scripture."

—**Kaitlyn Schiess**, author of *The Ballot and the Bible*

"Skye has written a Christ-exalting, clear, and compelling vision of the new heavens and new earth. How you view the future informs how you live in the present. Read this important book and gather with friends in a small group to explore the beauty of what our future holds."

—**Derwin L. Gray**, cofounder, Transformation Church; author of *God, Do You Hear Me?*

"In this accessible little book, Jethani masterfully translates critical theological insights about heaven into punchy, impactful, moving prose. These chapters are short enough to be used meditatively and devotionally, but sufficiently weighty and scholarly to help thoughtful Christians go deeper in biblical study and understanding. Best of all, Jethani makes Jesus, the kingdom of God, and the reign of heaven look beautiful, joyful, compelling, and liberating. If your experience of Christianity has been impoverished or even, at times, miserable, this book will offer aid and a luminous, sturdy hope."

—**Tish Harrison Warren**, Anglican priest and author of *Liturgy of the Ordinary* and *Prayer in the Night*

A VISUAL
GUIDE TO
EXPERIENCING
GOD'S KINGDOM
AMONG US

# WHAT IF JESUS WAS SERIOUS

## ABOUT HEAVEN?

## SKYE JETHANI

**Brazos**Press
*a division of Baker Publishing Group*
Grand Rapids, Michigan

Published by Brazos Press
a division of Baker Publishing Group
Grand Rapids, Michigan
www.brazospress.com

Printed in the United States of America

Library of Congress Cataloging-in-Publication Data
Names: Jethani, Skye, 1976– author.
Title: What if Jesus was serious about heaven : a visual guide to experiencing
    God's kingdom among us / Skye Jethani.
Description: Grand Rapids, Michigan : Brazos Press, a division of Baker
    Publishing Group, [2023] | Includes bibliographical references.
Identifiers: LCCN 2023014357 | ISBN 9781587436192 (paperback) | ISBN
    9781587436215 (casebound) | ISBN 9781493443994 (ebook) | ISBN
    9781493444007 (pdf)
Subjects: LCSH: Bible. Matthew.
Classification: LCC BS2576 .J48 2023 | DDC 226.2—dc23/eng/20230628
LC record available at https://lccn.loc.gov/2023014357

Baker Publishing Group publications use paper produced from sustainable forestry
practices and post-consumer waste whenever possible.

23   24   25   26   27   28   29      7   6   5   4   3   2   1

For Jay Patel
"There is a friend who
sticks closer than a brother."

# CONTENTS

Introduction: Redrawing Our Map of Heaven   9

**PART 1:** The Kingdom of Heaven Has Come Near   15

**PART 2:** The Kingdom of Heaven Is Like . . .   49

**PART 3:** Your Kingdom Come, Your Will Be Done on Earth
as It Is in Heaven   91

**PART 4:** I Am Going to Prepare a Place for You   125

**PART 5:** The Kingdom of the World Has Become the Kingdom
of Our Lord   159

Notes   189

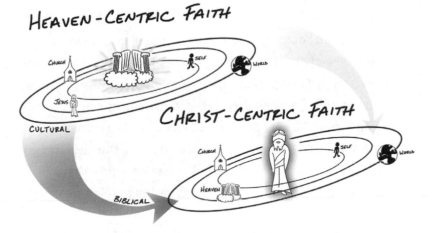

# INTRODUCTION

## REDRAWING OUR MAP OF HEAVEN

**MAPS FASCINATE ME.** Growing up, we had a giant *National Geographic* atlas the size of a coffee table. I used to flip the massive pages and wonder about the strange places on the other side of the planet. On the light-up globe in the den, I would try to measure with my hand how far where I lived in Chicago was from India, where my cousins lived. Even now, we have a map in our dining room marking all the places we've traveled as a family.

9

You may not be as enamored with maps as I am, but each of us carries them. I don't mean the app on your smartphone, but the maps you carry in your mind. Our mental maps provide a sense of geography to help us navigate between home, work, school, or the grocery store, but they do much more than that. They orient and guide us, offer perspective, and provide a framework for understanding our place in a complicated world. Our mental maps are imaginary models of the cosmos where we define what is real, what is important, and where things reside in relation to each other.

For example, our culture has shaped our minds to imagine the earth revolving around the sun. That is our mental map of the solar system, but people in most premodern cultures carried a vastly different mental map in which the sun revolved around the earth. In the sixteenth century, when Nicolaus Copernicus first presented evidence that the geocentric view of the cosmos was incorrect, many resisted changing their mental map. It was a long-held belief that humans were the climax and centerpiece of God's creation. Therefore, it made sense for the sun, moon, planets, and stars to rotate around us on a stationary earth. The desire to defend this established mental map was so intense that scientists were denounced as heretics for challenging it.

Today we refer to the shift from a geocentric to a heliocentric map of the solar system as the Copernican Revolution, and it reminds us that our mental maps don't always reflect reality and may need significant revision. When we encounter evidence that challenges our mental maps, we gain an opportunity to pause, evaluate, and revise our ideas. As Copernicus discovered, for some this process is uncomfortable or even terrifying because they foolishly equate their mental map of the world with the world itself. Therefore, any invitation to revise their map is viewed as an attack on reality itself that triggers fear, anger, and resistance. Revolutions, after all, never go unchallenged.

This is no less true for our *religious* mental maps. Consider what comes to mind when you hear the word *heaven*. Most modern Christians carry a culturally created mental map that imagines heaven as a distant celestial realm full of glorious dwellings occupied by the souls of God's redeemed people who are surrounded by angels in a paradise far removed from this earth. Our map also says the only path to heaven passes through death; it is utterly inaccessible to the living who still occupy the earth. For those shaped by popular forms of Christianity, our map also says that Jesus died on the cross so we might gain access to this heavenly paradise after we die.

Nearly everything about our faith—Jesus, the gospel, the cross, the church, our mission, even how we raise our children and interact with our non-Christian neighbors—revolves around the view of heaven I've just described. I don't think it's an exaggeration to say many of us have a heaven-centric mental map of Christianity. But what if our mental map is wrong? Just as the earth is not the center of the solar system, what if heaven is not the center of our faith?

As I noted earlier, we use maps to guide and orient ourselves. But if our maps are wrong, they are certain to *mis*guide and *mis*orient us. The same is true for our mental map of heaven. If it is incorrect, it will send other aspects of our faith and life off course as well. Significant parts of the Bible won't make sense to us, and we are likely to misinterpret even the most basic parts of Jesus's message and mission. I believe that is exactly what has happened in much of popular Christianity, and until we correct our mental map of heaven, we will find it extremely difficult to fix the other misaligned aspects of our faith.

Unfortunately, merely reading the Bible—while always a good practice—may not be enough to repair our warped view of heaven. This is because when we encounter the word *heaven* in the Scriptures, we insert our culturally created mental map. We rarely slow down long enough to ask whether our map of heaven and the Bible's are the same.

Because many people find great comfort in their culturally inherited map of heaven, any challenge to it is met with resistance or even accusations of heresy—not unlike what Copernicus faced when he asserted the earth revolved around the sun. Yet if we are going to be faithful to God, we must ask if our mental map of heaven is grounded in the revelation of Scripture or if it's mostly the product of cultural clichés and sentimental tradition. We must be willing to surrender the flawed map we *like* for the more accurate map we *need*.

## What Jesus Said about Heaven

After the work of scientists like Copernicus and Galileo, people slowly began to accept the heliocentric map of the solar system because their existing geocentric maps simply did not function as well. With the earth at the center, the observable movements of the planets made no sense and were unpredictable. But once they put the sun at the center, everything fell into place. The movement of the stars, moon, and planets in the sky became orderly and predictable. The heliocentric model found acceptance because *it worked*. The Copernican Revolution succeeded because it gave people a better, more reliable mental map of the universe.

My hope is that you have a similar experience reading this book. As we redefine heaven according to what the biblical authors wrote, and as we shift our mental map of Christianity from a heaven-centric to a Christ-centric vision, I trust that many other things will suddenly fall into place for you—from Jesus's sermons and healings to his death and second coming. When we come to embrace Jesus's map of heaven, we will discover that it works so much better than the one we've inherited from popular Christian culture.

In the pages that follow, we will explore what the Bible says about the kingdom of heaven with a focus on what Jesus and his apostles taught—and did not teach—about it. First, we will revise our mental map of heaven and God's kingdom (part 1). We will then use this new map to rethink the meaning of Jesus's parables (part 2) and miracles (part 3). After that, we will discover how the kingdom of heaven changes our view of the cross (part 4). Finally, we will explore what Jesus said about the ultimate fate of heaven and earth (part 5).

The process of redrawing your mental map of heaven will require you to rethink long-held assumptions, question previously unquestioned beliefs, and learn to read familiar passages from the Bible with new eyes. I'll warn you now, this is going to be disorienting and challenging, but revolutions always are. Let's begin.

# PART 1

# THE KINGDOM OF HEAVEN HAS COME NEAR

## MATTHEW 4:13–17

Leaving Nazareth, he went and lived in Capernaum, which was by the lake in the area of Zebulun and Naphtali—to fulfill what was said through the prophet Isaiah:

> "Land of Zebulun and land of Naphtali,
>     the Way of the Sea, beyond the Jordan,
>     Galilee of the Gentiles—
> the people living in darkness
>     have seen a great light;
> on those living in the land of the shadow of death
>     a light has dawned."

From that time on Jesus began to preach, "Repent, for the kingdom of heaven has come near."

How we define "Heaven"

"The Heavens" according to the Bible

God's dwelling

Sky + Space

Atmosphere

# ① IF JESUS WAS SERIOUS . . . THEN OUR VIEW OF HEAVEN MUST MATCH HIS

**THE FIRST CLUE THAT JESUS'S MAP** of heaven is different from ours is found in the word itself. The Hebrew word for "heaven" in the Old Testament is *shamayim*, and the Greek word in the New Testament is *ouranos*. Both words are plural and are usually accompanied by a definite article. Therefore, they should more accurately be translated into English as "the heavens." This means, according to the Bible, heaven is not a single place or a proper name, and we should not speak about heaven as a singular location the way we speak about London, Wrigley Field, or even something as vast as the Pacific Ocean.

The ancient cultures that shaped the Bible, and to which Jesus belonged, understood "the heavens" to be a vast realm surrounding the earth. First, they spoke of the heavens when referring to the sky or atmosphere. When Jesus said "the birds of the air," the actual language he used was "the birds of the heavens" (Matt. 6:26). The heavens are also where the celestial bodies abide—the sun, moon, and stars. Modern people distinguish between the atmosphere and outer space, but ancient cultures did not. Therefore, the heavens were simply everything in the air and above the earth.

"The heavens" also carried another important meaning in the ancient world. It referred to the dwelling place of God. The heavens are the invisible, intangible realm occupied by the Lord and his hosts. When this meaning is intended, our English Bibles will often ignore the plural Hebrew or Greek word and use the singular instead. For example, Isaiah 66:1 is translated as "This is what the LORD says: 'Heaven is my throne.'" When modern people read this verse with our mental map, it conjures images of God occupying a celestial city far away from the earth. But in Hebrew the verse says, "*The heavens* are my throne." The Lord is saying that he occupies the air/sky/atmosphere immediately surrounding us. Unfortunately, most of our translations of the Bible do not help us grasp this more immediate and accessible vision of God's heavenly presence.

The reason is simple. Our modern scientific knowledge has influenced how we translate these ancient texts. We want to differentiate the natural realm of the atmosphere from the supernatural realm of the spirits. Therefore, our English Bibles will say birds, clouds, thunder, or rain occupy "the air" but that God and his angels occupy "heaven," when all of these verses actually use the same plural word—"the heavens." By imposing our mental map of heaven onto the Bible, we obscure or erase the mental map of the biblical writers and of Jesus himself. Instead, we come to believe that heaven is a distant place accessible only after death and that God could not possibly be as near as the air filling our lungs.

The implications of this, as Dallas Willard notes, are a warped understanding of God, his kingdom, and the message of Jesus. "The damage done to our practical faith in Christ and in his government-at-hand by confusing heaven with a place in distant outer space, or even beyond space, is incalculable. Of course, God is there too. But instead of heaven and God also being always present with us, as Jesus shows them to be, we invariably take them to be located far away and, most likely, at a much later time—not here and not now."[1]

 **READ MORE: Acts 2:42–47; Ephesians 2:11–22**

## 2   IF JESUS WAS SERIOUS . . . THEN WE SHOULD FOCUS ON HEAVEN AND EARTH, NOT HEAVEN AND HELL

**"WHERE WILL YOU SPEND ETERNITY,** in heaven or hell?" That's a question Christians have sometimes used to start conversations with people outside the Christian faith, and it's one I heard frequently as a teenager when I was wrestling with questions about God and faith. Although asked with good intentions, those who employ this question are unaware that it contains dangerously skewed and profoundly unbiblical assumptions.

First, the question draws from our cultural map of heaven as a distant paradise for the dead. We've already explored how this does not align with the wider biblical vision of heaven as the atmosphere and beyond containing both visible (birds, clouds, sun) and invisible (God, angels, spirits) elements. Second, because the question assumes heaven is the abode of the righteous after death, it assumes that the opposite of heaven must be hell. "Heaven and hell" is such a popular phrase in our culture that, in our imagination, the two words seem to belong together like so many other natural opposites—good and evil, up and down, right and left, heaven and hell.

Yet the words *heaven* and *hell* never occur together anywhere in the Bible. Search in a Bible app or concordance for any variation of the phrase "heaven and hell" and you'll find no matches. As ubiquitous as the pair may be in our cultural discourse—both in and outside the church—the cultures from which the Bible emerged simply did not imagine heaven as the opposite of hell, and neither did Jesus.

Instead, the biblical authors spoke frequently about "heaven *and earth*." This phrase occurs dozens of times in both the Old and New Testaments as a way of describing the cosmos—the entirety of God's creation. In fact, this phrase is found in the very first sentence of the Bible: "In the beginning God created the heavens and the earth" (Gen. 1:1). This was the author's way of saying God created *everything*—seen and unseen, tangible and intangible, on the earth below and in the heavens above.

The phrase "heaven and earth" is also used to describe God's limitless power and dominion. The psalms often refer to God as "the Maker of heaven and earth" (see, e.g., Pss. 115:15; 121:2; 124:8; 134:3; 146:6). And Jesus prayed, "I praise you, Father, Lord of heaven and earth" (Matt. 11:25).

The Bible's frequent use of "heaven and earth"—and its non-use of our culture's preferred phrase "heaven and hell"—only makes sense if heaven is something more than an address in the afterlife. It is a present and accessible reality right now. It is both the atmosphere surrounding us and the invisible realm of God that is constantly interacting with us. Tim Mackie puts it this way: "The vision of reality in the scriptures is not even of heaven and earth as separate spaces but as overlapping spaces. The main storyline of the Bible is about heaven and earth interacting with each other. That's not on most people's radar. And it's strange because it's actually what the story of the Bible is about."[1]

Therefore, when someone asks, "Where will you spend eternity, in heaven or hell?" they are not simply confusing a cultural assumption for a biblical one. They are misrepresenting the point of the Bible and the message of Jesus. The primary emphasis of Scripture is not whether people will reside in heaven or hell after they die, but how heaven will be united with earth so that "God's dwelling place is now among the people" (Rev. 21:3).

 **READ MORE: Genesis 1:1–3; Acts 17:22–31**

"THIN" PLACES

OLD TESTAMENT

HEAVEN

TEMPLE

EARTH

NEW TESTAMENT

HEAVEN

JESUS

EARTH

## 3 IF JESUS WAS SERIOUS . . . THEN HE IS THE GATEWAY BETWEEN HEAVEN AND EARTH

**RATHER THAN A DISTANT PARADISE** for the dead, the biblical authors understood heaven to be an unseen realm alongside our own, and they believed that it interacted with our world the way the atmosphere interacts with the earth. They also believed these two realms—heaven and earth—could intersect and be occupied simultaneously. We see this in the opening chapters of the Bible:

the garden in Eden was the dwelling place of both people and God. There was no barrier between heaven and earth. After humanity rebelled against God, however, the two realms were separated, and the man and woman were prevented from entering back into God's heavenly space.

Throughout the Old Testament, this barrier was removed at special times and places. For example, in the patriarch Jacob's dream, angels ascended and descended a stairway between heaven and earth with the Lord himself at the top. When he awoke, Jacob said, "How awesome is this place! This is none other than the house of God; this is the gate of heaven" (Gen. 28:17). Jacob recognized the location as a point where the barrier between heaven and earth had disappeared and the two realms were accessible to each other. Celtic Christians referred to such locations as "thin places."

Of course, the Bible affirms that God is present everywhere and that even the heavens cannot contain him. Our ability to perceive God and the heavenly dimension is usually concealed the way a heavy curtain blocks sunshine. Sometimes the curtain between heaven and earth is peeled back, allowing light to pass through. Occasionally it is drawn open completely so that the glory of God fills our sight, as Jacob experienced in his vision at Bethel.

For God's ancient people, the most important thin place between heaven and earth was believed to exist in Jerusalem where the Israelites built their temple. It served as the gateway between heaven and earth, and the temple was where God could be directly encountered. Therefore, it was the centerpiece and focus of Israel's worship and communion with God. But in John's Gospel, Jesus announced that a new thin place between heaven and earth had arrived that would be a permanent opening between the two. A new and better temple had come.

According to the New Testament book of John, when Nathanael first encountered Jesus, he was amazed by his power and immediately called Jesus his "Rabbi," the "Son of God" and the "King of Israel." In response, Jesus assured Nathanael he hadn't seen anything yet: "Very truly I tell you, you will see 'heaven open, and the angels of God ascending and descending on' *the Son of Man*" (John 1:51). Jesus was directly referencing Jacob's vision at Bethel, the thin place where one could move between heaven and earth—between the realm of people and the presence of God.

Nathanael had correctly identified Jesus as Israel's true Messiah and King, but Jesus took things a giant step further by declaring he was also Israel's true *temple*. Remember, to the Jews at the time, the temple was the gateway to heaven—the thinnest of thin places where any barrier between the realm of humans and God disappeared. With his statement Jesus was substituting himself for Jacob's stairway; he was declaring himself to be the point where heaven and earth intersect and where divinity and humanity overlap. As Hans Urs von Balthasar writes, "In the Son, therefore, heaven is open to the world. He has opened the way from the one to the other and made exchange between the two possible, first and foremost through his Incarnation."[1]

In the Old Testament, we learn that heaven is not a faraway paradise but a realm alongside the earth and that sometimes the barrier between them can be thin or transparent. In the New Testament, we discover that Jesus himself is the point where heaven and earth overlap. He is the true temple and the permanent doorway that connects the two realms. This means that rather than looking to encounter God or experience the heavenly realm in a physical location, by climbing a mountain or by entering a sacred building, our access to both God and heaven is available to us right now through Jesus.

**READ MORE: Genesis 28:10–17; 1 Timothy 2:3–6**

ASSUMPTION...

REALITY...

KINGDOM OF GOD

YOU ARE HERE

YOU ARE HERE

## 4 IF JESUS WAS SERIOUS . . . THEN THE KINGDOM OF HEAVEN IS WITHIN OUR REACH

**SO FAR, WE'VE LEARNED** three important things about the biblical understanding, or map, of heaven. First, heaven is not a distant realm for the dearly departed but another dimension that exists alongside our own just as the atmosphere exists alongside the earth. Second, in the beginning, heaven and earth were united and the dwelling place of humans and God overlapped, but after our rebellion against God, heaven and earth were estranged. We no longer had direct access to God's heavenly realm.

Third, at some times and in certain places, the barrier between heaven and earth is thin, allowing us to catch glimpses of God's realm. In the Old Testament, the temple was believed to be the most important of these thin places, but in the New Testament Jesus declared himself to be the true and permanent gateway between heaven and earth. This brings us to the fourth critical way Jesus's map of heaven differs from ours. Our cultural assumption is that life in heaven is available only after death. But the centerpiece of Jesus's message was that life in heaven is accessible to us *now*.

Jesus began his public ministry with a simple but stunning announcement: "Repent, for the kingdom of heaven has come near" (Matt. 4:17). Other common translations say, "The kingdom of heaven is at hand." This is another case where our English translations often fail to convey Jesus's real meaning. We naturally assume that "at hand" or "near" means the kingdom of heaven is just around the corner, that it is *almost* here. But the word Jesus used conveys a completed action in the past. Eugene Peterson's paraphrase of Scripture in *The Message* gets it right: "God's kingdom *is here*" (emphasis added).

Jesus's original Jewish audience would have understood exactly what he was announcing. The Hebrew Scriptures had long prophesied about a coming age when heaven and earth would be reunited, when the whole earth would be filled with God's glory, when everything contrary to God's will would be swept away, when he would reign on the earth just as he reigns in heaven, and when the Lord and his people would dwell together as they had in the beginning. Jews in the first century referred to this coming age as "the kingdom of heaven" or "the kingdom of God." And the good news—literally, "the gospel"—that Jesus announced was that it had finally arrived.

There are two important things to understand about Jesus's announcement. First, Jesus was *not* saying a way had been opened for souls to escape from the earth to be with God in a heavenly paradise far away. In fact, he was announcing precisely the opposite—that God's presence and heavenly realm has arrived on earth. Heaven is "at hand"—finally within our reach, right now.

Second, Jesus did not announce that death was the gateway to the kingdom of heaven, as our culture assumes. Instead, he said heaven could be experienced right now if we "repent," which means to change direction or follow a different path. Remember, Jesus declared that he was the stairway between heaven and earth, and the true temple linking divinity and humanity. Therefore, we can enter the kingdom of heaven and experience life with God here on earth by turning from our current way of life to follow Jesus instead.

 **READ MORE: Mark 1:9–15; Matthew 4:13–17**

THE KINGDOM OF HEAVEN IS...

A)

B)

C)

D)

E) NONE OF THE ABOVE

## 5 IF JESUS WAS SERIOUS . . . THEN THE KINGDOM OF HEAVEN IS NOT THE CHURCH

**IN JESUS'S MOST FAMOUS SERMON,** found in Matthew chapters 5 through 7, he repeatedly speaks about the kingdom of heaven. In fact, he uses the phrase in the opening sentence: "Blessed are the poor in spirit, for theirs is the kingdom of heaven" (Matt. 5:3). The prominence of this kingdom language throughout Matthew's Gospel, and particularly within the Sermon on the

Mount, means that if we don't define the kingdom of heaven correctly, we are likely to misunderstand Jesus's entire message.

We've already seen that Jesus did not equate the word *heaven*
with a distant paradise for the deceased, as so many Christians
do today. But it is also common for modern Christians to incor-
rectly define the word *kingdom*. When these two words are put
together, the *kingdom of heaven* becomes a phrase primed for
misinterpretation.

In many Christian communities, and among those who read the
Bible uncritically, there is a long history of equating the kingdom
with the church. This may flow, in part, from the era of Christendom in which the structure of the church and the power of the
state were entwined. It was common to see political kingdoms and
spiritual authority as synonymous. Therefore, where the influence
of Christendom still lingers, people can assume the structures of
churches and the power wielded by church leaders are the manifestation of God's kingdom on earth.

Few Christians would identify their local congregation as "the
kingdom," but this language is often used when referring to col-
lections of churches—particularly when they cross sectarian or de-
nominational boundaries, as in, "Our pastor meets regularly with
the other ministers in town. He's very kingdom-minded." In this
case, "kingdom" is used to speak of the universal church rather
than a particular congregation or denomination. Drawing again
from political categories, if congregations are like local towns or

municipalities, and denominations are like states, some think of the kingdom like the federal government. It is the overarching authority that unifies all disparate expressions of the church.

But this definition of the kingdom of heaven cannot be what Jesus intended, and it is easily disproven. Returning to his Sermon on the Mount, swapping "the kingdom of heaven" with "the church" or even "the universal church" doesn't make sense in the context of Jesus's sayings. "Blessed are the poor in spirit, for theirs is *the church*"? Was Jesus promising those who are poor in spirit a position of high rank and control over assemblies of his followers? That interpretation is foreign to the New Testament, and you would also struggle to find it anywhere else in the early writings of the church. Unlike modern Christians, Jesus and his apostles never used the words *kingdom* and *church* interchangeably in the New Testament.

Therefore, we must be careful not to let popular Christian idioms and clichés lead us astray. The use of kingdom language when referring to the universal church may be well-intentioned; our goal may be to affirm Christ's presence and work among communities beyond our own. But when we use the word *kingdom* this way, we are straying from what Jesus meant and unintentionally diminishing the true magnitude and meaning of the kingdom of heaven.

**READ MORE: Matthew 5:3–12; Luke 17:20–21**

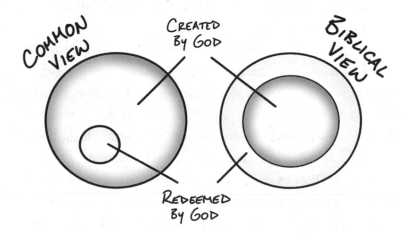

COMMON VIEW    CREATED By GOD    BIBLICAL VIEW

REDEEMED By GOD

## 6   IF JESUS WAS SERIOUS . . . THEN THE KINGDOM OF HEAVEN RESTORES ALL THINGS

**ASK MOST CHRISTIANS WHAT THE GOAL** of their faith is, and you're likely to hear something about spending eternity in heaven. As one well-known pastor summarized, "For most American Christians, the gospel is about getting my sins forgiven so I can go to heaven when I die."[1] In other words, many of us have a heaven-centric mental map of the Christian faith and the gospel itself. But how does that understanding conform to the New Testament's definition of the gospel?

A few years ago, New Testament scholar Scot McKnight wrote a book comparing our contemporary understanding of the gospel with the way Jesus and his apostles presented it. I was especially taken by his exploration of the book of Acts: "There are seven or eight gospel sermons or summaries of gospel sermons in the book of Acts. . . . If we have any Protestant bones in our body, we want to know what they gospeled and how they gospeled, and we want our gospeling to be rooted in and conformed to this gospeling."[2]

His point is simple. If we believe our faith should be defined by and emulate the faith of Jesus's apostles in the New Testament, then we must define the gospel how they defined it. Here's the remarkable part: In the eight gospel sermons recorded in the book of Acts, the apostles never mention anything about an afterlife in heaven or hell. Not once. Something has gotten off track if modern Christians think the ultimate goal of our faith is going to heaven while the earliest apostles never mentioned it in their own declarations of the faith.

This prompts an important question: If the goal of the gospel preached by Jesus and his apostles wasn't about the afterlife, what *was* the goal of their gospel? Peter's sermon in Acts 3 provides the answer. His message, which echoes Jesus's own preaching, crescendos with a vision of the future, when "the time comes for God to restore everything" (Acts 3:21). Peter is drawing heavily from his Old Testament Jewish tradition that emphasizes God's redemption of creation rather than our rescue from it. He envisions a day when God's realm (the heavens) and ours (the earth) are reunited as they were in the beginning.

Two things are worth highlighting. First, while so many modern gospel messages are about being rescued from an earth that is doomed, Peter's gospel sermon is about the earth being restored and redeemed. God's good news is not that we can escape to heaven. Instead, it is that through Christ, a world broken by sin, evil, and death will be repaired to the condition God always intended. It's a gospel of restoration, not merely rescue.

Second, Peter's sermon recognizes the wide scope of God's redemption. He says God will restore "everything." The good news is not limited to our immaterial souls or even to just humans. Through Jesus, the entire cosmos is being made right again, and that work will be completed when he returns from the heavens. For Jesus's apostles, the great hope of the gospel is not that we can escape *to* heaven but that Christ will return *from* heaven, restore the earth, and unite heaven and earth once and for all.

 **READ MORE: Acts 3:11–26; Romans 8:18–25**

PARENT          CHILD

## 7 IF JESUS WAS SERIOUS . . . THEN GOD GIVES US THE KINGDOM OF HEAVEN JOYFULLY

**OUR CULTURE HAS CONDITIONED US** to think of the kingdom of heaven like a celestial country club or posh gated community surrounded by slums. We assume the kingdom of heaven is an extravagant and exclusive residence for those special souls allowed to enter. We've already debunked part of this definition. The kingdom isn't where righteous souls go after death but rather our current reality where we encounter God's presence and accomplish his will. But how do we access this kingdom? Is it guarded by a fortified gate, and are there angelic bouncers to ensure no unworthy person sneaks in?

The guarded-country-club metaphor reflects the common assumption that God is a tyrannical judge perpetually disappointed by our shortcomings and failures. If that is God's character, it makes sense that he would reside in heaven behind an impenetrable wall, fortified gates, and armed security. These assumptions would also fuel the belief that anyone who does enter his kingdom must have done so by narrowly evading his wrath. Jesus, however, presents an entirely different vision of his heavenly kingdom that focuses on God's kindness rather than his anger.

In Luke 12, Jesus acknowledges that the world can appear dark and difficult, and these realities make us afraid. After listing common fears we all experience, Jesus tells his followers to abandon their worry and instead seek God's kingdom before anything else. In other words, we are to pursue God's presence first and not worry about the rest. Your Father knows what you need, Jesus said, and he will provide it for you.

What Jesus says next was life-changing for me: "Do not be afraid, little flock, for your Father has been pleased to give you the kingdom" (Luke 12:32). First, Jesus calls his followers his little flock. He is our Good Shepherd who cares for us, knows our name, and guides us through dark and dangerous places to safety.

Because he is our shepherd, we do not have to live in fear. The tenderness in these words contradicts the cold, judgmental vision of God so many of us carry.

But it gets better. Jesus then says the Father is *pleased* to give us the kingdom. Another translation (NASB 1995) says the Father "has chosen gladly" to make his kingdom available to us. In contrast to the popular view of God as a grumpy, strict gatekeeper, Jesus declares that God opens his kingdom to us joyfully. We don't have to pry the blessings of heaven from his hands or cajole him into being good toward us. He delights over us, and it brings him pleasure to give us the kingdom along with everything else that we need.

This is not an easy vision of God or his kingdom for many people to receive. I suspect that's because more of us struggle with believing in God's goodness than believing in God's existence. Surveys show nine out of ten Americans believe in God,[1] but far fewer actively worship him. Only 22 percent participate in a worship gathering weekly, and a majority of Americans seldom or never worship God.[2] The data suggests many people affirm God's existence, but they are less convinced about his benevolence. They don't see him as good enough to elicit their gratitude and praise with any regularity.

In a world of suffering and shadows, it is easy to doubt God's goodness. That is why we need to reflect more often on Jesus's words about the kingdom of heaven. Our heavenly Father wants us to know life with him, and he welcomes us with a smile. If we take Jesus's words seriously, will we dare imagine that God receives more pleasure from us than we are capable of receiving from him? And if providing for our needs and welcoming us into his kingdom brings joy to the Creator of the universe, what can possibly make us afraid?

**READ MORE: Luke 12:22–32; Psalm 23:1–6**

# WHAT IS "REDEMPTION"?

CREATION      EARTH      HEAVEN

RETURN      REMOVE

THE BIBLICAL VIEW      THE POPULAR VIEW

## 8 IF JESUS WAS SERIOUS . . . THEN REDEMPTION DOES NOT MEAN GOING TO HEAVEN

**REDEMPTION IS A COMMON BIBLICAL THEME,** and we engage with it regularly in our songs, prayers, and sermons. We speak a lot about God's redeeming power as a past, present, and future reality. For example, the Bible identifies Jesus's death on the cross as a "redeeming sacrifice" (past), numerous popular worship songs declare, "I am redeemed!" (present), and we preach about a coming age when God will redeem all our pain and sorrow (future). It is not an overstatement to say the entire Bible is about God's plan of redemption. But what exactly is God redeeming, and how does this relate to the kingdom of heaven?

The word *redemption* begins with the prefix *re-* meaning "again" or "return." It's a clue that any definition of *redemption* must look backward to a previous but currently unavailable state. It means to recover something that was lost or to restore something to its previous condition. A stolen car may be recovered or an old painting may be restored. In each of these examples, the object is brought back to a previous, better state of existence.

The same is true for the Christian theology of redemption. It is the restoration of our previous, intended condition. But to define what redemption means more fully, we must understand God's original intent for creation and for us. What were humans made for? Where did God intend for us to live? And what was lost when sin, evil, and death corrupted us and the world? Said another way—our theology of creation will determine our theology of redemption.

Yet much of contemporary Christianity ignores this critical link between creation and redemption. Some Christians hold strong beliefs about God's work of creation. They will argue about exactly *how* and *when* God created humans, then completely ignore *why* he created us when speaking about the nature of our redemption. If you ask most churchgoers what it means to be redeemed, their answer will likely involve "going to heaven." Contemporary

Christian mental maps paint an image of flying away to some spiritual paradise after death, but this vision of redemption looks nothing like the world God created in the beginning.

The early chapters of Genesis *do not* depict bodiless human souls living with God in a celestial heaven. Instead, we read about physical, embodied people inhabiting the *earth*. They rule there as God's representatives in perfect communion with him and one another. The intimate proximity of God with his people in the garden of Eden is the Bible's way of communicating the unity of heaven (God's realm) and earth (humanity's realm). It was a place of order, beauty, and abundance where heaven and earth were one.

Therefore, whenever Scripture talks about God's work of "redemption," it is describing the recovery and restoration of that original created order. Redemption means repairing the unity of heaven and earth, the intimate proximity of God and people, so that embodied humans can once again rule as God's representatives over his creation in perfect communion with him and one another.

Through Jesus and his life, we are given a glimpse of what this redemption looks like—the reunion of heaven and earth. Jesus described the kingdom of heaven with his parables, and he demonstrated its presence with his miracles. That is where we will turn our attention next.

 **READ MORE: Job 19:25–27; Romans 8:19–23**

# PART 2

# THE KINGDOM OF HEAVEN IS LIKE . . .

## MATTHEW 13:31-35

He told them another parable: "The kingdom of heaven is like a mustard seed, which a man took and planted in his field. Though it is the smallest of all seeds, yet when it grows, it is the largest of garden plants and becomes a tree, so that the birds come and perch in its branches."

He told them still another parable: "The kingdom of heaven is like yeast that a woman took and mixed into about sixty pounds of flour until it worked all through the dough."

Jesus spoke all these things to the crowd in parables; he did not say anything to them without using a parable. So was fulfilled what was spoken through the prophet:

"I will open my mouth in parables,
 I will utter things hidden since the creation of the world."

American Sermon Notes
Intro: Relevant Question
Point 1: Purpose
Point 2: Power
Point 3: Practical
Conclusion:
Application

Jesus's Sermon Notes
Explain (maybe later)

## 9 IF JESUS WAS SERIOUS . . . THEN WHY DID HE TEACH SO MYSTERIOUSLY ABOUT THE KINGDOM OF HEAVEN?

**DURING THE CLIMAX OF THE CLASSIC** courtroom movie *A Few Good Men*, the prosecutor demands to know the truth, and Jack Nicholson's character, Colonel Jessep, famously shouts back, "You can't handle the truth!"

Maybe he was right. Maybe most of us have a difficult time accepting the truth when it's presented to us directly. Emily Dickinson, the famous poet, seemed to think so: "The Truth must dazzle gradually / Or every man be blind." Therefore, rather than speaking plainly, she advises us to "Tell all the truth but tell it slant."[1]

That perfectly describes how Jesus taught about the kingdom of heaven. He spoke the truth about heaven, but he rarely spoke it plainly. Instead, he told it slant—indirectly, subtly, and often hidden in a story. As a result, some people missed his messages about the kingdom of heaven entirely. In this section, we'll explore some of the parables Jesus employed to explain the nature of God's kingdom, but in order to understand these stories, we must first acknowledge the enormous gap between Jesus's context and our own, between the way he taught the truth and the way we do.

Our modern, post-Enlightenment culture values clear, direct teaching. This is evident in what a lot of us look for from Sunday morning sermons. We want a sermon to include three points and practical, unambiguous applications. We hope to walk out of church on Sunday with more clarity about life and faith, not more questions. If the preacher manages to do that, we feel satisfied. If we regularly leave more confused than when we entered, the pastor might want to begin updating their résumé.

Jesus's first-century Jewish context was much different. It was a premodern culture that embedded wisdom into stories more often than it delineated truths with alliterated bullet points. This is what causes us to misinterpret and mishandle Jesus's parables about the kingdom of heaven. Our cultural instinct is to break his stories into their component parts and attach a clear meaning to each piece. We treat them as allegories or force them into a modern, didactic framework.

The uncomfortable fact is that Jesus offered little practical instruction in his sermons (at least as we define practicality today), and he never preached a popular "how-to" message. Jesus was not a straight talker. Instead, his stories were designed to challenge his listeners' assumptions and surprise them with unexpected, even offensive, revelations about God and his kingdom. Sometimes Jesus even *intended* to confuse his audience. Most often, however, his parables began with an object, circumstance, or relationship that his audience was familiar with, and then he surprised them with a twist that turned their assumptions upside down.

Gary Burge, a New Testament professor, describes Jesus's stories about the kingdom of heaven this way: "They are like a box that contains a spring—and when it is opened, the unexpected happens. They are like a trap that lures you into its world and then closes on you."[2] As we look at Jesus's parables about God's kingdom, be prepared to have many of your assumptions about heaven turned upside down as well.

 **READ MORE: Isaiah 29:15–21; Luke 18:31–34**

WHY WOULD ANYONE PICK "A"?

- BELIEF "B" IS A MYTH
- BROKEN SENSES OF SMELL, SIGHT, & TASTE
- INTERNET CONSPIRACY SAYS "B" IS POISON
- AN INABILITY TO MAKE GOOD DECISIONS

A   OR   B

## 10  IF JESUS WAS SERIOUS... THEN WHY DO SO MANY PEOPLE REJECT THE KINGDOM OF HEAVEN?

**LATER IN MATTHEW 13,** Jesus introduces two similar images to describe the response of those who discover the kingdom of heaven. In one he compares it to a man who finds a treasure in a field, and in the other to a merchant who discovers a pearl of great value. Both stories take an unfamiliar concept—the unseen realm of God's good reign—and compare it to familiar concepts from simple economics.

Any rational person would gladly give up something of little value to acquire something of great value. Likewise, Jesus demonstrates that the value of God's kingdom is so extraordinarily high that anything sacrificed for it ought to be released without hesitation. With these stories, Jesus is illustrating that the kingdom of heaven is an unbelievable bargain worthy of any sacrifice.

If that is the case, why do so many people still struggle to accept Jesus's invitation? There are two possible answers. First, people do not always act rationally. In fact, there is strong evidence that people will act irrationally and against their own self-interests even when they know they are doing so.[1] Our bent toward self-destructive and foolish choices confirms the Christian view that humans are universally corrupted by sin.

There is a second possibility, also rooted in the power of sin. Even if we are functioning rationally, we may not fully recognize the value of what is being offered to us because of our poor vision or ignorance. For example, when my son was young, he was addicted to sugar. But if I said to him, "Would you like crème brûlée?" he would have rejected the offer. He might assume it was the foreign name for some healthy vegetables or strange seafood—yuck! His response would be very different, however, if I explained that crème brûlée is vanilla pudding covered in sugar and cooked with a blowtorch. Having this knowledge and a clearer vision of the dessert would dramatically change his reaction.

Likewise, our blindness or ignorance about the kingdom of heaven prevents us from recognizing the true nature and value of what is being offered. As a result, we cling more tightly to what we have and dismiss the glories available to us through Christ. C. S. Lewis wrote about it this way:

> Indeed, if we consider the unblushing promises of reward and the staggering nature of the rewards promised in the Gospels, it would seem that Our Lord finds our desires, not too strong, but too weak. We are half-hearted creatures, fooling about with drink and sex and ambition when infinite joy is offered us, like an ignorant child who wants to go on making mud pies in a slum because he cannot imagine what is meant by the offer of a holiday at the sea. We are far too easily pleased.[2]

 **READ MORE: Matthew 13:44–46; Isaiah 5:20–21**

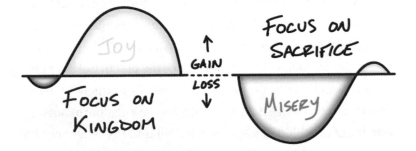

## 11 IF JESUS WAS SERIOUS ... THEN JOY, NOT MISERY, SHOULD MARK THOSE WHO ENTER THE KINGDOM OF HEAVEN

**RELIGIOUS PEOPLE USE** the word *sacrifice* a lot. Our modern dictionaries present two seemingly contradictory understandings for this term:

> (1) the surrender or destruction of something prized or desirable for the sake of something considered as having a higher or more pressing claim.

> (2) a loss incurred in selling something below its value.[1]

Both definitions are about loss and value, but the first emphasizes the greater value of what is gained, while the second focuses upon the value of what is lost. Whichever understanding of sacrifice we hold will deeply influence the practice of our faith.

As we discussed in the previous chapter, in Matthew 13, Jesus uses two brief, simple images to describe the kingdom of heaven. One is about a hidden treasure in a field and the other about a merchant searching for fine pearls. Both stories are about the unavoidable sacrifices necessary to acquire the kingdom, but in each parable, the emphasis is on the surpassing value of what is gained rather than mourning what was sacrificed to acquire it.

In some faith communities, sacrifice is almost entirely equated with loss—therefore it is the pain of a person's sacrifice that defines their righteousness. In such communities, the focus is upon how much you have given to God's work. How much you have suffered for God's mission. How much misery you are experiencing for the sake of God's kingdom. This view assumes that if your pain isn't excruciating, then your devotion isn't worth much. When religious people focus on what they've sacrificed to follow Jesus, they turn misery into a virtue.

In Jesus's stories about the treasure and the pearl, however, the central emotion of those who've acquired the kingdom of heaven is joy. The spotlight is upon what is *gained*, not upon what is *lost*. In fact, it's fair to assume the man who bought the field and the merchant who purchased the pearl experienced no misery at all.

Misery is sometimes a reality in our broken, evil world. As Jesus's cross shows us, it can be used by God for glorious and redemptive purposes. But misery itself is not to be admired as a sign of holiness or a mark of true devotion. Instead, those miserable Christians who mistake gloom for godliness ought to be most pitied. They are displaying an immature understanding of Christian faith. Rather than marveling at the joy of the kingdom of heaven that they have gained, they remain fixated on the far less valuable things of the world that they have lost.

 **READ MORE: Matthew 13:44–46; Mark 10:28–31**

ANCIENT JEWISH PARTY PLANNING

SAVE THE DATE + RSVP

PREPARATIONS

COME CELEBRATE!

PARTY

INVITATION 1

INVITATION 2

## 12 IF JESUS WAS SERIOUS . . . THEN GOD HAS CAREFULLY PREPARED A PLACE FOR YOU IN HIS KINGDOM

**WHILE JESUS WAS DINING** at the home of a religious leader, another guest said to him, "Blessed is the one who will eat at the feast in the kingdom of God" (Luke 14:15). A banquet or feast was a common image in ancient Israel to describe the age to come when heaven and earth are united under God's reign. It was how people in Jesus's culture described the kingdom of heaven. In language that's common among Christians today, the guest was saying, "Blessed is everyone who is saved!"

Jesus responded to this declaration in a strange way. He did not deny the blessedness of those who will share in God's banquet but instead told a parable that challenged popular assumptions about who will be at the table in God's heaven-on-earth kingdom. Jesus and his religious dinner guests had very different ideas about who was "saved." To understand Jesus's story, it's first helpful to understand more about banquets in his culture.

Because dynamics of honor and shame were utmost for households in ancient Israel, celebrations in a village were carefully scheduled to avoid conflicts. If a host held a banquet at the same time as another household, it would bring shame upon his neighbor as well as himself. Feasts scheduled at the same time would force guests to pick one or the other, thereby reducing the number of people able to attend each and resulting in dishonor for the hosts of both events.

To avoid this shameful situation, it was common for a host to send two invitations. The first invitation announced the banquet, ensured there were no competing events on the village calendar, and requested RSVPs from all the guests. It was the ancient equivalent of a "save the date" notice. With the date and guests determined, the host then began to prepare for the elaborate feast, a process that could take weeks. A second invitation was then sent when the banquet was ready to tell the guests to come and dine.

Jesus's parable emphasizes God's intentionality. Comparing the arrival of his kingdom to a banquet means the Lord, like a good host, has put thought, time, and care into ensuring that the arrival of his kingdom would not be a surprise and that his people would be ready to receive it. With this metaphor, Jesus is emphasizing how the kingdom of heaven is designed to be welcoming, a kingdom of inclusion rather than exclusion. The goal of the host is not to keep as many people *out* of the banquet as possible but to ensure everyone can join the party. That is the point of the dual invitations and the careful preparations.

Have you ever considered that God has planned and prepared for you to be with him? He is not indifferent about your presence at his table. He greatly desires to welcome and serve you. The kingdom of heaven has been carefully constructed as the realm where God can commune with you. In his kingdom you are not an afterthought, you are not a distraction, and you are never an interruption. This raises an important question: Are you intentional about your relationship with him? As we continue to look at Jesus's parable about the banquet, we'll discover how God responds to those who dishonor the gracious hospitality of his heavenly kingdom.

 **READ MORE: Luke 14:15–24; Mark 1:1–5**

SAY "YES" TO GOD

| RELIGIOUS HYPOCRITES (WORST)* | JOYFULLY RIGHTEOUS |

DISOBEY GOD ————————————— OBEY GOD

| HONESTLY UNRIGHTEOUS | RELUCTANTLY RIGHTEOUS |

\* SEE MATT. 21:28-32

SAY "NO" TO GOD

## 13 IF JESUS WAS SERIOUS . . . THEN REJECTING GOD'S KINGDOM IS BETTER THAN PRETENDING TO ENTER IT

**WE HAVE LOOKED AT HOW BANQUETS** were conducted in ancient Israel. A host would send two invitations. The first ensured there were no conflicting events planned in the community and asked guests to accept or respectfully decline the invitation. The second invitation was then sent once the banquet was prepared. This second invitation is what Jesus mentions in his parable: "At the time of the banquet [the host] sent his servant to tell those who had been invited, 'Come, for everything is now ready'" (Luke 14:17).

The meaning of the parable hangs on one important detail. The servant tells "those who had been invited" that the feast was ready. Jesus's audience would have understood that these people had received the first invitation and had already committed to attend the man's banquet. In the parable, however, the guests give the servant multiple excuses for not attending. They are trying to back out of their commitment.

Making things even worse, their excuses are ridiculous. Imagine RSVP'ing to attend a friend's all-expenses-paid wedding in Cabo San Lucas and then not showing up because you had to catch up on some email. That begins to capture the insult inflicted upon the host in Jesus's story and why he becomes so angry. The disrespect of the invited guests has brought great shame upon the host—a cultural violation we can barely comprehend in our modern context.

The parable is meant to show the difference between true and false devotion. Jesus told the story at a banquet of religious leaders deeply committed to keeping the Old Testament Law, which anticipated the coming of God's heavenly kingdom to earth. Metaphorically, through their religious observances, they had accepted

God's first invitation. Now, through Jesus, God was announcing that everything was ready, and his kingdom had arrived. But these devoutly religious men refused to enter the kingdom by welcoming and following Jesus. They were, like the guests in the parable, duplicitous in character and insulting to God.

The message remains relevant today. It is not enough for us to be religious, attend church, or participate in the rituals and sacraments of the faith—as good as those things may be. True devotion is not merely saying yes to God's invitation but actually showing up to be with him. Like the religious leaders of ancient Israel, a person may wish to be seen as devoted to God, but they may not want to submit themselves to a life under his reign. That is precisely what happens when we engage in external forms of religion but reject Jesus's presence and his commandments in our daily lives. In Jesus's view, it is more honorable to simply decline God's invitation outright than to offer him religious lip service. As we'll learn from the remainder of the parable, according to Jesus, it's better to be a heathen than a hypocrite.

 **READ MORE: Luke 14:15–24; Amos 5:21–24**

**3**

**WONDERS OF HEAVEN**

1: WHO _IS_ THERE

2: WHO IS _NOT_ THERE

3: THAT _I'M_ THERE!

(ACCORDING TO JOHN NEWTON)

**14** **IF JESUS WAS SERIOUS . . . THEN WE WILL BE SURPRISED BY WHO ENTERS THE KINGDOM OF HEAVEN**

**IN JESUS'S PARABLE,** after the invited guests made ridiculous and insulting excuses for not coming to the banquet, the host became angry. He then told his servant to instead fill his banquet with "the poor, the crippled, the blind and the lame" (Luke 14:21).

71

In ancient Israel, these people lived on the margins of society because they were assumed to be unrighteous and ungodly. It was popularly believed that their poverty or physical ailments were punishments from God for their sins. For the invited guests to have their places taken instead by people with far less social and religious status would have been humiliating—which was precisely the host's intention.

It got more interesting from there. The host then ordered his servant to "go out to the roads and country lanes and compel them to come in, so that my house will be full" (14:23). The man welcomed strangers from outside the village—likely Gentiles whom the Jews at the time saw as the lowest of the low. The host was declaring that his respectable neighbors who refused his banquet were worse than pagans. Ouch.

The real zinger, however, comes at the end of the parable. Jesus says, "I tell you, not one of those who were invited will get a taste of my banquet" (14:24). Most English readers will assume this is part of the parable and the host in the story is speaking, but the language shifts here to the plural tense, indicating that the voice is no longer that of the host speaking to the servant. Instead, many commentators believe these are the words of Jesus speaking directly to his audience.

Remember, Jesus told this parable in response to someone saying, "Blessed is everyone who will eat bread in the kingdom of God!" The culture equated eternal life with participation in God's celebration banquet at the end of history when heaven and earth are reunited. With his final statement, Jesus was boldly identifying God's banquet as his own. He was declaring himself to be God, the divine host, and warning Israel's religious leaders (the respectable invited guests) that they would never share his table. Instead, the places reserved for them would be given to sinners and outsiders.

Like Jesus's audience, we also make assumptions about who is a saint and who is a sinner. We think we can predict who will be welcomed at God's table and who will be rejected. This parable, however, should give us pause. John Newton, the repentant slave trader who composed the hymn *Amazing Grace*, wrote, "If I ever reach heaven, I expect to find three wonders there: First, to meet some I had not thought to see there; second, to miss some I had thought to meet there; and third, the greatest wonder of all, to find myself there!"[1]

 **READ MORE: Luke 14:15–24; Matthew 21:28–32**

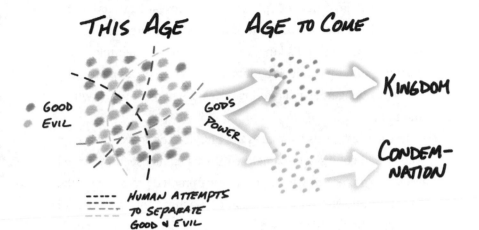

THIS AGE     AGE TO COME

- GOOD
- EVIL

GOD'S POWER

KINGDOM

CONDEM-
NATION

----- HUMAN ATTEMPTS
TO SEPARATE
GOOD & EVIL

## 15 IF JESUS WAS SERIOUS . . . THEN, FOR NOW, THE KINGDOM OF HEAVEN EXISTS ALONGSIDE THE KINGDOMS OF EVIL

**AMONG CASUAL READERS OF THE BIBLE,** there has been a long tradition of confusing the kingdom of heaven with the church. This was especially common during the era of Christendom in which European churches and state powers were enmeshed, and it persists today where people assume the organizational struc-tures of the church and the power wielded by church leaders are synonymous with God's kingdom. I have already debunked this misunderstanding of the kingdom, but its widespread popularity leads to a dangerous misreading of Jesus's parable of the wheat and the weeds.

In the story, Jesus compares the kingdom of heaven to a man who sowed good seed in a field while his enemy secretly sowed weeds. To protect the wheat from being uprooted prematurely, the weeds are allowed to grow alongside the wheat until the harvest. The man who sowed good seed says, "Let both grow together until the harvest. At that time I will tell the harvesters: First collect the weeds and tie them in bundles to be burned; then gather the wheat and bring it into my barn" (Matt. 13:30).

Those who equate the kingdom with the church have inter-preted this parable to mean that wicked, harmful people should be tolerated within the church alongside those seeking righ-teousness. In this interpretation, it is not appropriate to exercise church discipline or expel anyone for any reason. Such actions, they say, are reserved for God alone at the final judgment.

This view, however, is a complete misreading of Jesus's par-able. It requires one to ignore many other passages within the New Testament—and the words of Jesus himself—that call upon mature Christians to exercise discernment and discipline to protect the church from harm and guide everyone toward godliness. In its worst application, this reading of the parable has been an excuse for not removing corrupt or abusive church leaders.

The story of the wheat and the weeds is ultimately not about the church but about the world. We occupy an age in which the kingdom of heaven and its righteousness has taken root. It is here, among us, growing and expanding. But its presence is not without resistance. Alongside God's kingdom is also the evil of the world. Until the harvest, we must expect the goodness of God's kingdom and the evil of the world to coexist alongside, and in tension with, each other. But the fact that evil persists in the world is never an excuse for the followers of Jesus to ignore it within their own community or to silence those who have been wounded by agents of the church.

**READ MORE: Matthew 13:24–43; 1 Corinthians 5:6–13**

## THE PROBLEM OF EVIL

IF GOD IS ALL-GOOD & ALL-POWERFUL, WHY IS THERE EVIL IN THE WORLD?

ANSWERS

GOD DOES NOT EXIST

GOD IS NOT ALL GOOD OR POWERFUL

(GOOD DOES NOT EXIST EITHER)

EVIL DOES NOT REALLY EXIST

MY KINGDOM HAS OVERCOME EVIL WITH GOOD

## 16 IF JESUS WAS SERIOUS . . . THEN EVIL IS A REAL PROBLEM THAT WILL BE OVERCOME BY THE KINGDOM OF HEAVEN

**ONE OF THE MOST PERSISTENT** challenges to faith is what philosophers call the Problem of Evil. The problem is easy to understand but much harder to solve. It says, If God is all-powerful and all-good, why is there so much evil in the world? This sets up three possible, but unsatisfying, solutions:

1. God is good but not all-powerful and therefore unable to stop evil.
2. God is all-powerful and could stop evil but chooses not to and is therefore not good.
3. God does not exist.

Some skeptics engage the Problem of Evil by observing the world around them. Stephen Fry, a famous British comedian and atheist, was asked what he would say to God if he discovered after death that God existed. Fry answered, "How dare you create a world in which there is such misery that is not our fault? It's not right. It's utterly, utterly evil. Why should I respect a capricious, mean-minded, stupid God who creates a world which is so full of injustice and pain?"[1] Fry went on to talk about bone cancer in children and parasites in people's eyes—all manner of inexplicably terrible things.

For others, the Problem of Evil is deeply personal. Russell Baker was a well-known columnist for *The New York Times* and wrote frequently about his childhood. His father died when he was a boy, and Baker said, "After this, I never cried again with any real conviction, nor expected much of anyone's God except indifference."[2]

Every worldview, including non-religious ones, must address our universal experience of evil. Some do this by ignoring God, like Baker. Others address evil by denying God's existence altogether, like Fry. But in their attempts to solve the Problem of Evil, these answers unknowingly create another problem. As celebrity atheist

Richard Dawkins admits, without God there is "no evil, no good, nothing but pitiless indifference."[3] In other words, most attempts at solving the Problem of Evil create an inverse dilemma—the Problem of Good. How do we explain the existence of goodness, justice, and hope in a cosmos *without* God?

Some approaches resolve the Problem of Evil by denying the reality of evil altogether. Evil doesn't actually exist, they say, because what we call evil is merely the absence of good the way darkness is the absence of light. Some Eastern philosophies go a step further by dismissing the suffering caused by evil as merely an illusion one must transcend.

Christian faith is different. While affirming the existence of an all-powerful, all-loving Creator, it also acknowledges the real presence of evil in the world. This seemingly paradoxical vision is what Jesus's parable of the wheat and the weeds illustrates. Good and evil are real and exist in this age side by side—a truth that is self-evident to most people. The parable does not explain *why* evil exists but instead draws our attention to the coming harvest, when it will be removed, root and branch, and destroyed forever. For me, this is one of the more appealing aspects of Jesus's teachings about the kingdom of heaven. Unlike others, he fully acknowledges and sympathizes with our experience of evil while also offering us hope for the day when it will be overcome by good.

**READ MORE: Matthew 13:24–43; Revelation 21:1–4**

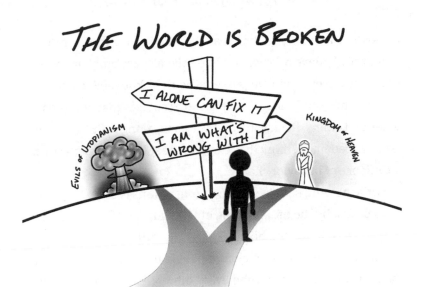

## 17 IF JESUS WAS SERIOUS . . . THEN WE SHOULD NOT CONFUSE HEAVEN'S POWER WITH HUMAN POWER

**AN EPISODE OF THE FREAKONOMICS RADIO** podcast focused on a team of brilliant researchers competing for a $100 million grant. The prize will be given to the group with the best idea for curing one social problem anywhere in the world. Angela

Duckworth and Katy Milkman are competing for the grant because they believe they've identified the biggest problem in the world—us. Even when we possess the right knowledge and resources, they say, humans still make bad choices that hurt themselves and others. Duckworth and Milkman, along with an all-star team of academics, think they can find the solution by perfecting the science of behavior change.

While helping people make better decisions is a worthy goal, I was struck by the utopian tone of the podcast. "Could solving this one problem," the host asked, "solve all the others?"[1] If a system were developed to ensure people made wise decisions, the podcast speculated, then every other great dilemma could be solved—including poverty, climate change, and even terrorism. Perfecting behavioral change through science was framed as the silver bullet of human progress, the ultimate tool to vanquish our depravity and bring lasting peace and prosperity to the world.

Despite their lofty goal, I'm certain that what plagues humanity is beyond the healing power of professors—even ones with $100 million. The project is just the latest example of a reoccurring modern dream: the eradication of evil through human ingenuity and social progress. Karl Marx tried with enforced economic equality. Adolf Hitler tried through racial purity. Even Walt Disney tried with his "Experimental Prototype Community of Tomorrow" (aka EPCOT).

Combating the effects of evil and solving the world's problems is a calling we ought to embrace. Pursuing God's will on earth as it is in heaven is what citizens of the kingdom of heaven do. But Jesus makes clear in his parable of the wheat and the weeds that our efforts alone will never fully eliminate evil. The final work of uprooting evil will happen when God's power is unleashed over all of creation at the end of the age. History shows that when humans arrogantly assume we possess this divine vocation, when we believe we can make a perfect world, rather than solving the problem of evil we become part of it.

 **READ MORE: Matthew 13:24–43; 1 Corinthians 15:24–28**

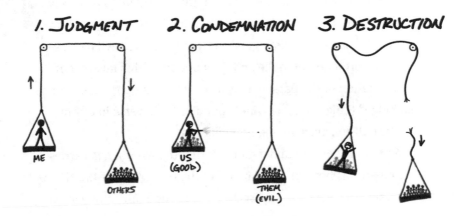

1. JUDGMENT    2. CONDEMNATION    3. DESTRUCTION

ME

OTHERS

US (GOOD)

THEM (EVIL)

### 18 IF JESUS WAS SERIOUS . . . THEN CITIZENS OF THE KINGDOM OF HEAVEN DO NOT CONDEMN OTHERS

**WE'VE ALREADY SEEN** that Jesus's parable of the wheat and the weeds explains how the good seed of God's kingdom is inter-mingled with the bad seed sown by the enemy and that utopian ideas about the world are misguided because the righteous and the wicked will occupy the earth together—at least for now. Some have misunderstood the story to mean that we ought to passively accept evil in this age and patiently wait for the final judgment or that we do not need to distinguish between good and evil because God will sort it all out in the end. Proponents of this laissez-faire interpretation of the parable may also cite Jesus's command "do not judge" (Luke 6:37)—a widely popular Bible verse in our pluralistic culture, even among nonbelievers.

What this view misunderstands is that the word *judge* carries two meanings both in English and in the Greek text of the New Testament. It can mean "to discern" or "to condemn." When Jesus says, "Do not judge," he is not calling us to cease from discerning between good and evil. Rather, he is calling us to not condemn others, and he makes this clear in Luke 6. Immediately after saying, "Do not judge, and you will not be judged," he says, "Do not condemn, and you will not be condemned" (v. 37). Repeating the same idea with slightly different language was common among Hebrew teachers to add emphasis and clarity.

Jesus is telling us not to pass final judgment or declare a person irretrievably guilty. Citizens of God's kingdom are called to discern but never devalue. This is implied in Jesus's parable. Discernment is essential to distinguish the wheat from the weeds. However, uprooting and destroying the weeds (i.e., condemning them) is not our role. That task is reserved for God at the end of the age.

To condemn a person means to declare them worthless; to say they do not matter to anyone including God. The instinct to condemn others is rooted in a desire to elevate ourselves. We think that by cutting someone down we can be lifted up, that our ascension depends on another's subjugation. In this way, a person who frequently condemns others is actually displaying their own insecurity, fragility, and self-doubt.

Jesus's parable reveals the foolishness of such a person. Pulling the weeds early will result in accidentally pulling the wheat as well; in the same way, when we take over God's responsibility to make final judgments on evil in the world, we inflict more harm. Instead, we are to use discernment to distinguish the weeds from the wheat and then patiently await God's judgment as we withhold condemnation.

Destroying the weeds prematurely, Jesus says, will also destroy the wheat. A crusade to end all evil will invariably end many good things in the process. It is a subtle but important lesson—when we become zealous in our condemnation of others, we unknowingly condemn ourselves.

**READ MORE: Matthew 13:24–43; Luke 6:37–38**

# PART 3

# YOUR KINGDOM COME, YOUR WILL BE DONE ON EARTH AS IT IS IN HEAVEN

## LUKE 4:16–21

He went to Nazareth, where he had been brought up, and on the Sabbath day he went into the synagogue, as was his custom. He stood up to read, and the scroll of the prophet Isaiah was handed to him. Unrolling it, he found the place where it is written:

> "The Spirit of the Lord is on me,
>     because he has anointed me
>         to proclaim good news to the poor.
> He has sent me to proclaim freedom for the prisoners
>         and recovery of sight for the blind,
>     to set the oppressed free,
>         to proclaim the year of the Lord's favor."

Then he rolled up the scroll, gave it back to the attendant and sat down. The eyes of everyone in the synagogue were fastened on him. He began by saying to them, "Today this scripture is fulfilled in your hearing."

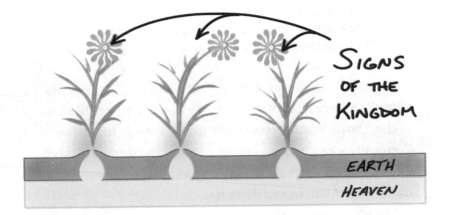

Signs OF THE Kingdom

EARTH

HEAVEN

## (19) IF JESUS WAS SERIOUS . . . THEN MIRACLES ARE SIGNS THAT THE KINGDOM OF HEAVEN IS AMONG US

**IN C. S. LEWIS'S CLASSIC** children's book *The Lion, the Witch and the Wardrobe*, the land of Narnia had fallen under the curse of the White Witch. It was perpetually winter, but a prophecy foretold that the true king would return and the curse would be broken:

Wrong will be right, when Aslan comes in sight,
At the sound of his roar, sorrow will be no more,
When he bares his teeth, winter meets its death,
And when he shakes his mane, we shall have spring again.[1]

In one scene, Edmund noticed the Witch's sleigh was having difficulty moving through the snow. The air was warmer, the snow wetter, and he heard the sound of running water in the distance. Eventually leaves began to appear on trees, and patches of green grass peeked through the snow. The curse was breaking. Spring had arrived. Aslan was on the move!

Lewis's allegory wonderfully illustrates the state of our world. Like Narnia, things are not as they should be. Our world lies under a curse of evil, sin, chaos, and death, which is contrary to God's nature and his intent for creation. When Jesus arrived, he announced this perpetual winter had been broken and spring was at hand. "The time has come. The kingdom of God has come near" (Mark 1:15), he proclaimed. Reading from the scroll of Isaiah at the synagogue, Jesus announced that the arrival of God's heavenly kingdom on earth would break the curse and "set the oppressed free" (Luke 4:18).

After declaring this good news, Jesus began to do wonders—he healed the sick, fed the hungry, liberated the possessed, and restored sight to the blind. He manifested the presence of heaven and broke the curse of sin and death everywhere he went. When asked by what power he accomplished these signs and what they

94

meant, Jesus said, "the kingdom of God has come upon you" (Luke 11:20). Just as Aslan's arrival in Lewis's story caused the first green shoots of spring to break through the snow, the arrival of Jesus caused the first signs of heaven's reign to break through the disorder, ugliness, and scarcity of our sinful world. We sometimes call these signs miracles.

Contrary to the modern view that defines a miracle as an event that *violates* the natural order, in the Gospels, a miracle is an event that *restores* the proper order—the order God always intended. With this understanding, we see that evil, injustice, and death are the real intruders, and miracles are the signs that God is putting his world back to rights. They are the evidence that God is reuniting his presence with his people and ensuring that his will is done on earth as it is in the heavens.

Of course, like the transition from winter to spring, sometimes these signs are subtle and sometimes they are dramatic. Warming air may cause a frozen stream to thaw slowly, almost imperceptibly. Or it may cause a mountain of glacial ice to calve with a thunderous sound into the sea and trigger a tsunami.

Likewise, the presence of the kingdom of heaven is often revealed gently and subtly through forgiveness, generosity, patience, and mercy. The ice thaws as we overcome prejudices, embrace the poor, and practice hospitality toward strangers. But sometimes the kingdom of heaven crashes upon the world with dramatic and inexplicable power. Sometimes the freeze of winter doesn't melt slowly; it is forcefully shattered in events we perceive as miracles.

 **READ MORE:** Luke 11:14–20; Matthew 15:29–31

GOD'S KINGDOM IS SEEN IN THE ORDINARY & THE SPECTACULAR

ERROR OF CESSATIONISM

ERROR OF SPECTACULARISM

NEVER

ROUTINELY

MIRACLES HAPPEN...

## 20 IF JESUS WAS SERIOUS . . . THEN WE MUST AVOID TWO MISTAKES ABOUT MIRACLES

**THE GOSPELS OFFER A COMPELLING** and integrated vision of miracles as sudden manifestations of the kingdom of heaven. They restore rather than violate the divine order of the world. Using the Chronicles of Narnia analogy of the White Witch's curse of perpetual winter, we've seen that the coming of God's kingdom is like the arrival of spring. The thaw is gradual and often imperceptible (a theme found in many of Jesus's parables about the kingdom), but sometimes the ice melts with sudden effect and thunderous impact. These more dramatic demonstrations of God's kingdom are what we call miracles.

Before we turn our attention to some of these stories, we need to recognize two common mistakes Christians make regarding miracles. The first is the error of cessationism. This is the view that the miraculous signs and gifts evident in Jesus's ministry and the early church have ceased and no longer occur today. There are different forms of cessationism, with some arguing miracles may happen today but only where the church is not established or where the gospel is unknown. This view emerges from the belief that miracles serve as divine PR. As one cessationist said, "The primary function of these gifts was to accredit the gospel message, confirming that Jesus was both Lord and Christ."[1] But once that message is received and the church is established, miracles are no longer necessary.

However, this view ignores that many of Jesus's miracles were not accompanied by any preaching or declaration of his identity, and sometimes he even performed miracles in strict secrecy. That's extremely odd if the primary function of these signs was to validate his message and identity. But if these wonders are manifestations of God's kingdom breaking into the world to reunite heaven and earth and reverse the power of sin, evil, and death, then they carry meaning all by themselves apart from any teaching or preaching being present. And since the kingdom of heaven is continuing to turn the curse of winter into the glory of spring, there's no reason to think that this ongoing transformation won't sometimes be spectacular even in our day and culture.

On the opposite end of the spectrum from cessationism is an error I call spectacularism. As the name implies, it's a form of faith that fixates upon and comes to expect the spectacular. Christians caught in this error will emphasize that miracles should be common occurrences and normative for all believers. Dramatic manifestations of spiritual power, they say, ought to happen all the time, and they will look for these conspicuous signs, both to authenticate their own faith and to identify godly leaders. Unlike more biblically informed traditions that value the gifts of the Holy Spirit and say miracles may happen as a manifestation of God's kingdom, spectacularism preaches they *must* happen—and frequently. It's like misidentifying a spring thunderstorm with spring itself and believing the absence of thunder and lightning means spring hasn't yet arrived—despite the more subtle evidence all around.

Jesus and his apostles did not emphasize miracles as the only, or even the best, evidence of God's kingdom. A person who appears to perform miracles isn't necessarily an agent of heaven filled with God's Spirit (see Matt. 7:21–23). Instead, Scripture calls us to look for the less spectacular signs of heaven's presence—the good fruit that emerges slowly from a person's life and character.

Likewise, Jesus sometimes denied the crowds demanding to see more miracles because their fixation on the spectacular was causing them to miss the more enduring signs of God's kingdom, and he saved his most shocking warning for those focused on spectacular acts of power rather than true obedience to God's will.

As we begin to explore the stories of Jesus's miracles, we must avoid the errors of both extreme cessationism and extreme spectacularism. The former says the kingdom of heaven is only revealed subtly, and the latter says it's only revealed spectacularly. But God's kingdom, like the warmth of spring, is a gracious mix of both.

 **READ MORE: Matthew 7:13–23; 1 Corinthians 13:1–13**

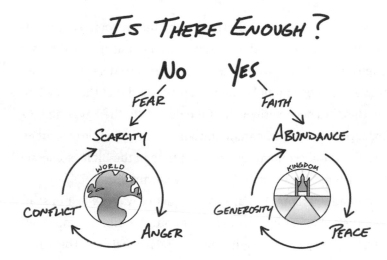

## 21 IF JESUS WAS SERIOUS...
## THEN THE KINGDOM OF
## HEAVEN CONFRONTS OUR
## FEAR OF SCARCITY

**THE OLD TESTAMENT SCHOLAR** Walter Brueggemann made an observation that has transformed the way I read the Bible. In the Old Testament book of Exodus, Pharaoh was concerned that the Hebrews living in Egypt were becoming too numerous. He viewed them as a threat to his power and the prosperity of his empire. Pharaoh subjugated the Hebrews by making them slaves, but when they continued to increase in number, he ordered the murder of every Hebrew infant boy. Pharaoh believed that the growth of the Hebrews necessarily meant the decline of the Egyptians. As Brueggemann said, "Pharaoh introduces the principle of scarcity into the world economy. For the first time in the Bible, someone says, 'There's not enough. Let's get everything.'"[1]

Behind Pharaoh's brutality and injustice was the fear of scarcity. It's a theme that occurs throughout the Bible, throughout human history, and that still plagues modern societies. The fear of not having enough can even explain modern political and cultural movements. For example, two Harvard Business School professors, Michael Norton and Samuel Sommers, researched why so many white Americans felt they were being left behind economically when the data showed whites still outearned every other group in the country. Their findings made headlines. As Sommers explained, "It turns out that the average white person views racism as a zero-sum game. If things are getting better for Black people, it must be at the expense of white people."[2]

At the time of their research, racial minorities had increasing visibility in the culture, elite institutions were more diverse than ever before, and America had just elected its first Black president. Like Pharaoh's fear that if the Hebrews prospered then the Egyptians could not, the data showed that a growing number of white

Americans believed their prosperity required denying prosperity to people of color. Heather McGhee argues this zero-sum view is "at the root of our country's dysfunction. . . . There's an us and a them, and what's good for them is bad for us."[3] Or, as Brueggemann said, there is a scarcity of wealth, power, and resources, and because there's not enough for everyone we must fight to get as much as we can.

This scarcity mindset always leads to paranoia and injustice. It causes the powerful to fear and oppress the powerless, just as we see in the story of Exodus. But this common feature of the world's empires exists in stark contrast to the kingdom of heaven.

Unlike the fear of scarcity that drove Pharaoh, Israel experienced the reality of God's abundance. He provided water from rocks and bread from heaven while his people wandered in the wilderness. From the creation account onward, the presence of the Lord was always accompanied by an abundance of resources so that everything and everyone could flourish. Where God and his kingdom are present, where heaven and earth overlap, there is always enough. Therefore, fear is unnecessary, and rather than seeing others as competitors for a limited supply of resources, we are set free to embrace others as friends and welcome them as companions to share the unending fountain of heaven's provision.

It's this biblical contrast between scarcity and abundance, between the world's empires and the kingdom of heaven, that must inform how we read the stories of Jesus feeding the multitudes.

Each story begins with the problem of scarcity—the disciples face thousands of hungry people but have only a few loaves and fish. How will so little feed so many? In each story, this scarcity causes the disciples anxiety and even anger. While they don't exhibit the same paranoid evil as Pharaoh, their fear represents the first steps down that dark path. But Jesus intervenes and shows them another way: "Taking the five loaves and the two fish and looking up to heaven, he gave thanks and broke the loaves. Then he gave them to his disciples to distribute to the people. He also divided the two fish among them all. They all ate and were satisfied" (Mark 6:41–42).

The empires of this world are driven by scarcity. They convince us to be afraid, to feel threatened by others. They teach us to justify our selfishness and greed. And when they have fully shaped our imaginations and affections, as they did to Pharaoh, they turn us into agents of evil who will endorse any injustice to keep our family, tribe, or nation safe and prosperous. That is not the way of Jesus. Heaven is not a zero-sum kingdom of winners and losers, but rather a kingdom of abundance where there is always more than enough for everyone.

 **READ MORE: Mark 6:30–44; Exodus 1:8–16**

KINGDOM vs. CONSUMERISM

## 22 IF JESUS WAS SERIOUS . . . THEN ABUNDANCE IS ABOUT GOD'S KINGDOM, NOT OUR CONSUMER DESIRES

**MANY OF JESUS'S MIRACLES** display the abundance that marks the presence of the kingdom of heaven. His first miracle recorded in the Gospels was providing an abundance of wine to a wedding feast. Jesus called his first disciples after producing a miraculous catch of fish so large it nearly sank Peter's boat. More than once, Jesus multiplied a few fish and loaves to feed a multitude of hungry people.

Throughout the Bible, abundance is always linked to the presence of God, going all the way back to the garden in Eden and the numerous Old Testament stories of God's abundant provision for his people in the wilderness. Jesus's Jewish disciples certainly recalled these stories when they saw him produce an overflow of wine, fish, and bread. These miracles of abundance were signs of God's presence and the arrival of heaven's kingdom on earth.

Unfortunately, that's not the lens through which many modern people see these miracles. Instead, we often view the miracles of abundance through our cultural lens of consumerism—a capitalist mindset of having and wanting more stuff. This leads to a different, and distorted, interpretation of these signs. The miraculous catch of fish, for example, is a favorite story among both preachers and followers of the "prosperity gospel." This uniquely American heresy, which has now been exported around the globe, links Christian faith with earthly, material, and especially financial success. In a nutshell, it preaches that God wants you to be rich.

Sometimes the prosperity gospel is overt and brazen—like the television preacher who said, "Do you want a hundredfold return on your money? Give and let God multiply it back to you. No bank in the world offers this kind of return! Praise the Lord!"[1] More often, however, the prosperity gospel prefers a more subtle disguise. It seeps into our imaginations and the practice of our faith almost imperceptibly as we absorb the values, assumptions, and habits of our consumer culture. It's the lie behind the lie that God always wants us to be safe and comfortable, that suffering is abnormal, and that every setback or struggle in our lives is due to a lack of faith. The prosperity gospel is active when we negotiate with God in our prayers by promising him X if he will bless us with Y, or whenever we seek to use Jesus to achieve some other desire—whether financial prosperity, political or cultural power, professional success, or even missional impact.

Before you dismiss this as a fringe element in the church, consider that a *TIME* magazine poll found that 17 percent of US Christians explicitly embrace the prosperity gospel, 31 percent agree that "if you give your money to God, God will bless you with more money," and 61 percent agree that "God wants people to be prosperous."[2] 61 percent! The prosperity gospel is far from fringe; it's widely accepted in the American church. When those shaped by it read the story of the miraculous catch of fish, they see a story that verifies their belief that Jesus is the key to material success. After all, look what he did for Peter's fishing business! Not only does this interpretation ignore the long literary theme of abundance from the Old Testament, but it also fails to see the nuances at work in Luke's telling of the story and the context of the miracle itself.

Consider the sequence of events. Jesus got into Simon Peter's boat "and asked him to put out a little from shore. Then he sat down and taught the people from the boat" (Luke 5:3). Jesus cast out his message of God's kingdom; he was fishing for followers from the fishermen's boat. When he finished, Jesus told Simon to again "put out" his boat into the water and let down his nets (5:4). There is a linguistic link between what Jesus did from the boat—teach the people—and what Simon does from the boat—catch fish. After the miraculous catch, Jesus makes the implicit link explicit. He tells Simon, "from now on you will fish for people" (5:10). Jesus calls Simon to copy what he's been doing—proclaiming the kingdom of heaven and watching as multitudes are miraculously gathered through Jesus's power.

Once we see the catch of fish in this context and with Luke's literary clues, we see that the story has nothing to do with material prosperity or Jesus blessing Simon's business. Instead, it's a sign of God's presence that also foreshadows Simon's vocation of widely proclaiming the kingdom of heaven to multitudes who will put their faith in Jesus.

 **READ MORE: Luke 5:1–11; John 2:1–11**

KINGDOM'S
PACE

WORLD'S
PACE

UNHURRIED
WIDE VIEW
ABUNDANT TIME
GOAL:
    WALKING WITH
    GOD

HURRIED
NARROW FOCUS
SCARCE TIME
GOAL:
    ACHIEVING FOR
    GOD

## 23 IF JESUS WAS SERIOUS . . . THEN LIFE IN THE KINGDOM OF HEAVEN DOESN'T HURRY

**LET'S TRY AN IRREVERENT THOUGHT EXPERIMENT.** Imagine you're the Messiah, the incarnate presence of God on earth. Given the world's great needs and your great power, how would you manage your time? I imagine most of us, being shaped by modern values, would think about efficiency and impact and develop a strategic plan to maximize our desired outcomes. We'd probably operate with a sense of urgency to accomplish as much as possible. Our culture teaches us to think about time as a limited and scarce resource.

Now consider how Jesus managed his time. First, he stayed for only about thirty years, and he used only about ten percent of that time to teach, heal, and reveal the kingdom of heaven. Instead, he spent most of his time on earth in obscurity working as a carpenter. That doesn't seem very efficient. During his three years of public ministry, Jesus occupied most of his time with the least influential people at the bottom of society rather than the movers and shakers at the top where his message could have reached more people more quickly. Even as he lived and served among the lower classes, Jesus still regularly escaped from the crowds to be alone—sometimes for weeks at a time.

When reading the Gospels, you start to notice that Jesus did not move with a sense of urgency. As John Ortberg writes, "Jesus was often busy, but he was never hurried."[1] This is evident in the story of the hemorrhaging woman in Mark 5. Jesus and his disciples were on their way to the home of a synagogue official named Jairus whose daughter was dying. This detail is important because it adds a sense of urgency to the story and explains why the disciples were frustrated when Jesus stopped amid the crowd. You can imagine the twelve rolling their eyes when Jesus asked, "Who touched me?"

"What do you mean, 'Who touched me?'" the disciples might have replied. "Everyone is touching you! We're stuck in this crowd, and we need to get to Jairus's daughter before she dies. Stop asking silly questions, Jesus, and let's go!"

But Jesus sensed that someone in the crowd needed his attention. Rather than rushing with his disciples, rather than being carried along by the crowd, rather than feeling the urgency of those around him or the scarcity of time, Jesus stopped. He understood that his ministry wasn't only ahead of him at Jairus's house; it was also right there in the crowd. Jesus slowed down long enough to engage with an outcast woman whose faith had given her remarkable courage. He blessed her, affirmed her faith, confirmed her healing, and gave her the dignity of his attention and time.

Unlike many of us, Jesus wasn't so fixated on the future that he missed an opportunity to manifest the kingdom of heaven in the present. Because he wasn't driven by an unrelenting urgency to achieve something, he was able to give his attention to what his Father was doing at each moment and with each person he encountered. This kind of deep communion with God and undistracted awareness of the present is possible only when we do not rush. Carl Jung once said, "Hurry is not of the devil; hurry is the devil."[2] John Mark Comer elaborated on this observation in his book *The Ruthless Elimination of Hurry*. He wrote, "Corrie ten Boom once said that if the devil can't make you sin, he'll make you busy. There's truth in that. Both sin and busyness have the exact same effect—they cut off your connection to God, to other people, and even to your own soul."[3]

Obviously, Jesus's miracles happened because he was connected to God, but we overlook how many miracles happened because he was deeply aware of the people around him. He paid attention to a man with a withered hand on the Sabbath. Jesus heard the shouts for mercy from a blind man whom the people tried to keep quiet as he passed by. And he felt the touch of one woman who reached out to him in faith amid a crushing crowd. All these wonders were possible because Jesus didn't hurry. Everywhere and in every moment, he was fully present with God and with others. That is what life in the kingdom of heaven looks like.

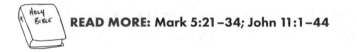 **READ MORE: Mark 5:21–34; John 11:1–44**

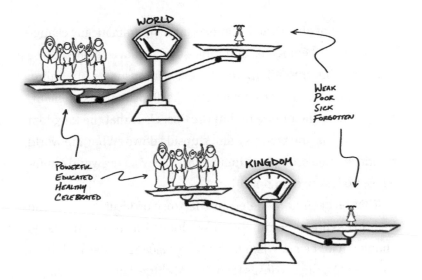

## 24  IF JESUS WAS SERIOUS . . . THEN IN THE KINGDOM OF HEAVEN THE LAST WILL BE FIRST

**SEVERAL TIMES, WHEN SPEAKING** about the kingdom of heaven, Jesus said, "Many who are first will be last, and the last first" (Mark 10:31; Luke 13:30). But what on earth does that mean? Does "first" and "last" refer to time, as in the sequence of things? Or, is Jesus using "first" and "last" in reference to status? Is he talking about a person's rank? Adding to the complication, Jesus uses this phrase in different contexts that may dramatically change its meaning. Theologians and Bible scholars have debated these matters of interpretation, but there is consensus on one thing. Regardless of what Jesus meant specifically with this statement, the general principle we find in the Gospels is that the kingdom of heaven flips the world's values upside down. What the world prioritizes, God's kingdom diminishes. And what the world diminishes, God's kingdom prioritizes.

This reversal is modeled in the story of Jesus healing the hemorrhaging woman, which we looked at in the previous chapter. It all began when Jairus, a synagogue leader with high social status, came to Jesus for help. "My little daughter is dying," he said. "Please come and put your hands on her so that she will be healed and live" (Mark 5:23). Jairus was desperate and no doubt full of fear, but he was also a man of high status and significant power. Therefore, he sought Jesus's help boldly and directly. And Jesus agreed to go with him.

As they headed to Jairus's home, Jesus encountered another fearful, desperate person seeking his healing touch. Unlike Jairus, however, the bleeding woman occupied the opposite end of the social hierarchy. She approached Jesus differently. She came toward him secretly and in silence, hoping to go unnoticed. It didn't work. Jesus felt power leave him when she touched the edge of his robe and was healed, and he immediately looked for who was responsible. Exposed for her irreverent and profane act—the law forbids an "unclean" woman from touching anyone—she confessed what she had done. Rather than responding with anger or condemnation, however, Jesus affirmed her faith and blessed her.

There's another detail in Jesus's response that we should consider. He addressed the woman as "daughter." It's an odd choice given the woman's age—she was likely older than Jesus based on the details of her condition—and because Jesus never addressed any other woman as "daughter" in any Gospel account. So why does he use such an affectionate and tender term for this older, ostracized woman? Once again, it's all about context.

Remember, Jesus was on his way to heal the daughter of a synagogue leader. Jairus was an important man with an important position. This identity afforded Jairus, and therefore his daughter, privilege and priority in society. As we already noted, the bleeding woman was the opposite. She had no advantage and had been societally discarded. Yet Jesus dignified her by stopping to heal and bless her *first*. He elevated her value by giving her the privileged identity of being his "daughter." It's as if Jesus were saying, "I will come and heal the synagogue leader's daughter, but first I will heal my own daughter—the one who has been rejected by the world."

The story is a subtle but powerful reversal of expectations. In no way does the story criticize Jairus. He was a loving father desperate for his daughter's healing. But unlike Jairus's daughter, the hemorrhaging woman had no one to advocate for her. No one to help her. No one on her side. Jesus did not reject Jairus's request, but he prioritized God's child in the street rather than the synagogue leader's child in the house, because in the kingdom of heaven the last will be first, and the first will be last.

 **READ MORE:** Mark 5:21–43

MIRACULOUS FEEDING
MARK 6:30-44

5,000 FED
+
5 LOAVES
+
12 BASKETS
_____
ISRAEL

OLD TESTAMENT
REFERENCE

5 BOOKS OF
THE LAW

12 TRIBES
OF ISRAEL

## 25 IF JESUS WAS SERIOUS . . . THEN THE KINGDOM OF HEAVEN IS THE FULFILLMENT OF ISRAEL'S STORY

**EVERY FAMILY WITH YOUNG CHILDREN** has its own lexicon, a set of words or phrases familiar to those inside the family but usually meaningless, or even bizarre, to outsiders. For example, when my oldest daughter was a toddler, she called her favorite blanket "mitme." For the next decade, everyone in our home referred to their favorite bedtime animal or blanket as their "mitme." A guest in our home would have no idea what that meant, but within the culture of our family the word was entirely familiar and immediately understood. The same phenomenon exists within wider cultures. Certain words or phrases have clear insider significance that may be unclear to or entirely lost on those from outside the culture.

For example, if I wrote a poem that included the phrase "life, liberty, and the pursuit of happiness," most Americans would recognize it as a reference to the Declaration of Independence and conclude that my poem was about the United States. However, that connection might go unnoticed by a non-American. Or, if I composed a short story that incorporated the phrases, "I have a bad feeling about this," "It's a trap!" "Never tell me the odds," and "Stay on target," nerds would immediately know that I was deliberately connecting my story to *Star Wars*. Someone unfamiliar with George Lucas's galaxy far, far away, however, would completely miss those references and their layers of meaning.

Likewise, both Jesus's parables and miracles about the kingdom of heaven are loaded with this kind of coded cultural language that first-century readers would have immediately understood but which often flies right over our heads. The miraculous feeding of the five thousand in Mark 6, for example, is deliberately told with multiple Old Testament references to Israel.

When Jesus saw the large crowd, "he had compassion on them, because they were like sheep without a shepherd" (Mark 6:34).

Israel's greatest leaders, Moses and David, were both shepherds. Before Moses died, he asked the Lord to raise up another leader so that the people "will not be like sheep without a shepherd" (Num. 27:17). Both Jeremiah and Ezekiel prophesied that the coming Messiah would lead Israel like a good shepherd.

Continuing the Moses motif, Jesus tried to escape into a remote place, but the people followed him there, just as the people had followed Moses into the wilderness. And just as Moses had miraculously fed God's people in the desert with heavenly bread and meat, Jesus miraculously fed his followers in the wilderness by multiplying fish and loaves.

The Gospel writer also highlights specific numbers that often carry symbolic meaning in the Bible. The people were fed with five loaves of bread, just as Moses gave Israel the five books of the Law. The twelve baskets of leftovers correspond to the twelve tribes of Israel.

Unlike the feeding of the four thousand, which we read about later in Mark's Gospel (and we'll discuss in the next chapter), in the story of Jesus feeding the five thousand, only the men were counted, and they were seated in groups of fifty and one hundred. This is the language of military formations like the preparation of Israel's armies before entering the Promised Land.

Finally, the story concludes by emphasizing that everyone ate and was "satisfied." Again, this detail seems insignificant to us, but it's another callback to Moses, Israel's deliverance, and the

Promised Land, a place where God's people will eat and be satisfied (Deut. 8:10).

What is Mark saying to us with all these details, symbolic numbers, and Old Testament references? To his first-century readers the message would have been undeniably clear—through Jesus, God is accomplishing a new exodus. Jesus is the Lord's Shepherd that Moses and the prophets foresaw. He is the true Deliverer leading the people out of bondage. He is the new Lawgiver, and he is preparing God's people to overcome their enemies and enter a new kind of Promised Land—the kingdom of heaven. Everything in Israel's history and Scriptures has been leading up to this moment and this person. Jesus is fulfilling God's purpose for Israel. Through him the kingdom of heaven has come to the earth.

 **READ MORE: Mark 6:30–44**

MIRACULOUS FEEDING          OLD TESTAMENT
MARK 8:1-13                 REFERENCE

4,000 FED                   4 CORNERS
+                             OF THE EARTH
7 LOAVES
+                           7 DAYS OF
7 BASKETS                     CREATION
_____

GENTILES

(26) IF JESUS WAS SERIOUS ...
THEN THE KINGDOM OF HEAVEN
WILL WELCOME PEOPLE FROM
EVERY NATION

**JUST TWO CHAPTERS AFTER THE STORY** of Jesus feeding the
five thousand, there is another, very similar story in Mark 8. Once
again, a large crowd was following Jesus, they had nothing to eat,
and Jesus had compassion for them. Like before, Jesus miraculously fed them with just a few loaves and fish, and his disciples

collected baskets full of leftovers. The obvious question is, Why did Mark include these two nearly identical stories in his Gospel? One insufficient answer is that Mark was simply recording what happened. There were two miraculous feedings of two large crowds, so he wrote about both events.

This answer isn't satisfactory because it assumes that Mark intended to write down everything Jesus did in his public ministry. We know that isn't the case. There are many stories, parables, and teachings of Jesus recorded by Matthew, Luke, and John that Mark excluded from his account. Likewise, another Gospel writer plainly said that Jesus did many more things that were not written down (see John 21:25). So, we know that Mark intentionally selected only certain stories and organized them in his Gospel to make a particular point about Jesus and his kingdom. This brings us back to our original question: Why did Mark intentionally include two nearly identical miraculous feedings in his Gospel?

We can discover the answer in the context of the second feeding. The two stories that precede it in Mark's Gospel are about Jesus healing Gentiles (non-Jews). First, a Syrophoenician woman begged Jesus to heal her daughter. Jews at the time often referred to Gentiles as "dogs"—a derogatory and dehumanizing insult. Despite her non-Jewish identity, the woman said, "even the dogs under the table eat the children's crumbs" (Mark 7:28). For her persistence and faith, Jesus healed the woman's daughter. Immediately after this, Jesus entered the predominantly Gentile region of the Decapolis and healed a man who was deaf and mute (Mark 7:31–37). Both stories show a gradual transition from Jesus revealing the kingdom of heaven exclusively among Jewish communities to manifesting his kingdom among Gentiles. This is where Mark situates the miraculous feeding of the four thousand.

We've already explored how the feeding of the five thousand in Mark 6 was full of references to the exodus, Moses, and the fulfillment of Israel's story. But none of those Israel-specific words, symbols, or numbers are repeated in the miraculous feeding of the four thousand. Instead, they are exchanged for Gentile-specific symbols.

For example, in Mark 6 the number five is repeated. Jesus fed five thousand by multiplying five loaves, a reference to the five scrolls of the Torah given to Moses, and they collected twelve baskets of leftovers, which links to the twelve tribes of Israel. In Mark 8, rather than five and twelve, the numbers four and seven are repeated. Jesus multiplied seven loaves and they collected seven baskets of leftovers. Seven is associated with the seven days of creation—an event involving the whole world, not just Israel. Likewise, in this second feeding, Jesus fed four thousand people. The number four is linked throughout the Bible to the four corners of the earth, an all-inclusive image of the nations. Jewish law also identified four laws Gentiles within Israel were required to follow (see Lev. 17:8, 10–13; 18:26). If the first miraculous feeding screamed "Israel!" the second miraculous feeding shouted "Gentiles!"

Once we see the miracle's context, location, and symbols, we can begin to understand why Mark included it. The first miraculous feeding was Mark's way of showing that God's heavenly kingdom had arrived through Jesus as the fulfillment of Israel's history. That alone was surprising and wonderful news, but with this second miraculous feeding, Mark was making an even more shocking claim. Through Jesus, the kingdom of heaven had also arrived among the Gentiles.

First, Jesus healed a Gentile woman's daughter from a distance, then he healed a Gentile man by touching him, and finally, he displayed the abundance of God's kingdom among the Gentiles by miraculously feeding them, just as the Lord had miraculously fed Israel in the wilderness. With these stories, Mark was carefully addressing the most contentious controversy in the early church—the uniting of Jews and Gentiles into one new community of God through Christ.

The feeding of the four thousand is a reminder to us that Jesus and his kingdom are not limited by our expectations or cultural prejudices. The kingdom of heaven is at work even among those we consider below us, those who we may regard as subhuman, unworthy, or even our enemies. If you've constructed a vision of Christianity that says heaven's favor, abundance, and blessing are exclusively for people like you, that's a sure sign your imagination has been shaped more by the divisions of the world than by the kingdom of heaven.

**READ MORE: Mark 7:24–37; Mark 8:1–13**

# PART 4

# I AM GOING TO PREPARE A PLACE FOR YOU

## JOHN 14:1-12

"Do not let your hearts be troubled. You believe in God; believe also in me. My Father's house has many rooms; if that were not so, would I have told you that I am going there to prepare a place for you? And if I go and prepare a place for you, I will come back and take you to be with me that you also may be where I am. You know the way to the place where I am going."

Thomas said to him, "Lord, we don't know where you are going, so how can we know the way?"

Jesus answered, "I am the way and the truth and the life. No one comes to the Father except through me. If you really know me, you will know my Father as well. From now on, you do know him and have seen him."

Philip said, "Lord, show us the Father and that will be enough for us."

Jesus answered: "Don't you know me, Philip, even after I have been among you such a long time? Anyone who has seen me has seen the Father. How can you say, 'Show us the Father'? Don't you believe that I am in the Father, and that the Father is in me? The words I say to you I do not speak on my own authority. Rather, it is the Father, living in me, who is doing his work. Believe me when I say that I am in the Father and the Father is in me; or at least believe on the evidence of the works themselves. Very truly I tell you, whoever believes in me will do the works I have been doing, and they will do even greater things than these, because I am going to the Father."

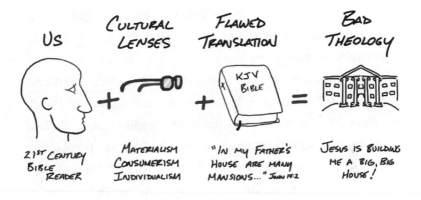

US

CULTURAL LENSES

FLAWED TRANSLATION

BAD THEOLOGY

KJV BIBLE

21ST CENTURY BIBLE READER

MATERIALISM CONSUMERISM INDIVIDUALISM

"IN MY FATHER'S HOUSE ARE MANY MANSIONS..." John 14:2

JESUS IS BUILDING ME A BIG, BIG HOUSE!

## 27 IF JESUS WAS SERIOUS . . . THEN HE'S NOT BUILDING YOU A MANSION IN HEAVEN

**POPULAR CULTURE,** both inside and outside the church, has long equated heaven with the afterlife, the place where some people go when they die, despite the lack of biblical support for this view. As we've already seen, the apostles never spoke about heaven in any of their gospel sermons, and the "kingdom of heaven" carried a different meaning in Jesus's culture and for his first disciples—one that had no connection to a distant spiritual paradise for the dead. In fact, the Bible has shockingly little to say about what happens to us immediately after we die, and what it does say doesn't reference heaven.

Paul affirms that "to be away from the body" is to be "at home with the Lord" (2 Cor. 5:8). Jesus told the criminal beside him on the cross, "Today you will be with me in paradise" (Luke 23:43). Apart from these rather generic yet comforting statements, the New Testament ignores any description of the afterlife, preferring instead to focus on the ultimate fate of all creation when the dead will be resurrected, Christ's enemies vanquished, and all things incorporated into God's kingdom. (Part 5 will delve into these themes.)

The Bible's silence about what happens between our physical death and future resurrection at Christ's return should be a clue that it's not very important. Therefore, when we come to the Bible demanding to know about the afterlife in heaven, we are asking a question the biblical authors never intended to answer. The contemporary Christian marketplace, however, is eager to meet this demand by selling books by authors claiming to have returned from the hereafter.

Known within the publishing industry as "heaven tourism," the genre has sold millions of copies and spawned numerous bestsellers, multiple movies, and a fair number of lawsuits when some authors were exposed for fabricating their accounts. In 2015, one of the largest Christian retailers stopped selling heaven tourism books because of concerns they were replacing "the sufficiency of biblical revelation."[1] Others, sadly, remain committed to the genre because it is so profitable despite being overtly unbiblical.

Some heaven tourism books try to win Christian approval by grounding their vision of the afterlife in Jesus's words from John 14. On the night before his death, he spoke to his disciples about his Father's house having many rooms and that he was going to prepare a place for them. For centuries, the King James Version, which poorly translated "many rooms" in John 14:2 as "many mansions," contributed to believers viewing heaven as a celestial subdivision with golden streets and gilded homes that would make rappers, professional athletes, and social media influencers jealous. Therefore, when Jesus said, "I go to prepare a place for you," Christians assumed he ascended into heaven to oversee the greatest real estate development project in the universe. However, once we correct the KJV translation and shed our cultural assumptions about the afterlife, we will discover Jesus was not talking about heaven at all.

The word for "rooms" or "mansions" in John 14:2 is difficult to translate because it occurs only one other time in the New Testament, just a few verses later. In John 14:23, Jesus says the Father and Son will make their "home" or "dwelling" within those who obey his commands. Here, the word has nothing to do with houses, rooms, or mansions. It simply means *where one resides*, and the context eliminates the silly idea that Jesus literally builds a structure inside our bodies for him and the Father to occupy. It's clear he is speaking metaphorically about the intimacy that will exist between the Father, Son, and those who obey their words. The same is true earlier in the same conversation when he promises to prepare a place for his disciples.

Remember, the disciples were confused and distraught about Jesus's announcement that he was leaving them. His words about preparing a place for them in his Father's house were meant to alleviate their anxiety. These verses are not about heaven, which Jesus never mentions anywhere in his Farewell Discourse.[2] They are about Jesus promising his frightened friends they would dwell with him forever in God's presence. John 14, like the Gospel itself, isn't about heaven; it's about living in never-ending union with God.

 **READ MORE: John 14:1–14; John 15:1–5**

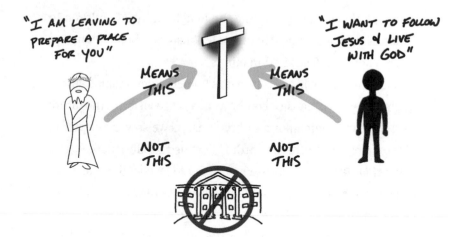

## 28 IF JESUS WAS SERIOUS . . . THEN THE CROSS IS HOW HE HAS PREPARED A PLACE FOR US WITH GOD

**THE NIGHT BEFORE HIS CRUCIFIXION,** Jesus told his disciples he was leaving "to prepare a place for you" (John 14:2). As we've discussed, this is widely misunderstood to mean that Jesus was leaving earth to build a heavenly paradise with gold streets and gilded mansions for his followers to inhabit after they die.

Although this idea might ignite the imaginations of children in Sunday school and appeal to the materialism of religious consumers, it's not what Jesus had in mind.

Still, this view of Jesus as heaven's homebuilder remains attractive in large part because it conforms nicely to a vision of the future held by many contemporary Christians. As we saw in chapter 6, it's common to believe the earth is destined for destruction, and when that time comes, those belonging to Jesus will be rescued off the sinking ship and resettled in the shiny new place he's currently constructing. I've already explained why this pop theology is riddled with problems that contradict the message of the New Testament. It also causes us to completely miss the point of Jesus's farewell conversation with his disciples.

In John's Gospel, whenever Jesus talks about leaving his disciples, returning to his Father, or being lifted up or glorified, they are all different ways of speaking about the same event: his death and resurrection. When Jesus told his disciples, "I go to prepare a place for you," it does not mean that *after* he leaves via the cross, he'll begin his next project of preparing a place for them. Rather, Jesus is saying that his departure by way of the cross *is precisely how* he will prepare a place for them. Jesus's leaving and his preparing are not two events that will happen *sequentially* (leave first and then prepare a place), but the same events happening *simultaneously*. Jesus will not prepare a place for his disciples with God *after* his death and resurrection but *through* his death and resurrection.

The fact that so many Christians read these verses—which are all about Jesus's looming death—and ignore the cross to instead focus on heaven (which he never mentions!) reveals how we hold on to our cultural map of heaven as we read the Bible. Our fixation on the glories of heaven and disdain for the agonies of the cross are why we assume Jesus is talking about a heavenly construction project when in truth he is pointing the disciples, and us, to his far greater accomplishment through the cross. Like the Gospels themselves, our faith would be much stronger if we spent less time wondering about the architecture of heaven and far more time contemplating the glories of the cross.

 **READ MORE: Colossians 1:15–20; 2 Corinthians 5:14–21**

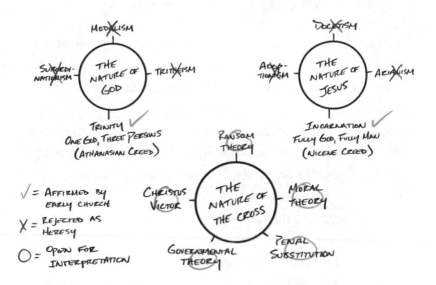

MODALISM

SUBORDI-NATIONISM — THE NATURE OF GOD — TRITHEISM

TRINITY ✓
ONE GOD, THREE PERSONS
(ATHANASIAN CREED)

DOCETISM

ADOP-TIONISM — THE NATURE OF JESUS — ARIANISM

INCARNATION ✓
FULLY GOD, FULLY MAN
(NICENE CREED)

✓ = AFFIRMED BY EARLY CHURCH

✗ = REJECTED AS HERESY

O = OPEN FOR INTERPRETATION

RANSOM THEORY

CHRISTUS VICTOR — THE NATURE OF THE CROSS — MORAL THEORY

GOVERNMENTAL THEORY

PENAL SUBSTITUTION

## 29 IF JESUS WAS SERIOUS . . . THEN THERE ARE MANY WAYS TO INTERPRET WHAT HE ACCOMPLISHED ON THE CROSS

**EARLY CHRISTIANITY WAS RIDDLED** with controversies. As the message of Jesus spread, first through his apostles and then others, it encountered other philosophies, religions, and cultures throughout the Roman Empire. In some cases, these foreign ideas

135

and values were congruent with the gospel and incorporated into the growing church. Some of these non-Christian ideas, however, were plainly contrary to the gospel and contaminated the original message Jesus and his apostles preached. This messy stew of orthodox and unorthodox beliefs created a patchwork of Christian doctrines throughout the world and led to fierce disagreements among Christians about which doctrines aligned with the true gospel.

Contributing to the controversy was the ambiguity of Scripture itself. Some critical ideas were never explicitly delineated by Jesus's teaching or the apostles' writings—at least not in a single place—making it possible for divergent interpretations to emerge. Two of the most divisive issues for the early church were the nature of God (what exactly was the relationship between God the Father, Son, and Holy Spirit) and the nature of Jesus (what exactly was the relationship between his humanity and divinity).

With dozens of false teachings infecting the church, eventually councils of theologians and church leaders from across the Roman Empire were assembled to determine what the Scriptures truly affirmed and what they clearly refuted on these matters. The councils codified the Bible's teaching about the Trinity (one God existing eternally as three persons) and the nature of Jesus (fully human and fully divine). Since the early centuries of the church, any departure from these biblical and church-affirmed doctrines has been deemed unorthodox and a rejection of the true faith.

What does this have to do with the cross and the kingdom of heaven? Over the centuries, Christians have held many different understandings of Jesus's death, how it relates to God's kingdom, what goals his death achieved, and how precisely it achieved them. Even today some Christians disagree bitterly over which "theory" of the crucifixion is right or which view ought to be at the center of the message we proclaim.

For example, some strongly believe that one particular understanding of the cross, known as "penal substitutionary atonement," is synonymous with the gospel itself. Others, while affirming the biblical truth of substitutionary atonement, argue for a broader definition of the gospel. Fellowships are still bonded or broken over this issue.

Unlike the nature of the Trinity or Jesus, however, no church council was ever convened to clarify the nature of the cross or how precisely God reconciled "to himself all things, whether things on earth or things in heaven" through Jesus's death on it (Col. 1:20). No creed was written to determine which single understanding of the cross was correct, because the New Testament does not affirm just one. Like a gem whose facets reflect light differently as it turns, our vision of the cross changes as we see it from the different perspectives recorded in Scripture. No single view negates all others. When the many facets of the cross are embraced together, we begin to marvel at the beauty and mystery of what God has done through Christ on it.

 **READ MORE:** Hebrews 2:14–18; Romans 5:16–19

THE WORLD SEES DEFEAT    GLORY    THE CHURCH SEES VICTORY

SCANDAL

## (30) IF JESUS WAS SERIOUS . . . THEN HEAVEN'S ENEMIES WERE DEFEATED THROUGH THE CROSS

**WHEN READING THE GOSPELS CAREFULLY,** two things become apparent. First, Jesus spoke a lot about the kingdom of heaven. As we've seen, it was the centerpiece of the message he preached, the focus of the parables he taught, and even the explanation for many of the miracles he performed.

Second, the Gospels spend a significant amount of time focused on Jesus's death. About 40 percent of the Gospels of Matthew,

Mark, and Luke tell about the final days of Jesus's life, and John's Gospel increases this to 66 percent.[1] Clearly, the Gospel writers believed the crucifixion of Jesus was critically important. But how does the cross fit with the kingdom? What is the link between these two dominant Gospel themes?

Many of us have been taught to see Jesus's death through the lens of individual salvation. His sacrifice liberated us from our slavery to sin, and by paying the penalty for our evil, Jesus both atoned for it and opened the way for our reconciliation with God. This is a good and true vision of the cross, and it resonates with us because, like virtually everything else in our culture, it conforms to hyperindividualism. It says the cross is primarily about *my* salvation, *my* atonement, and *my* sin.

The Bible, however, presents the cross as more than an instrument of individual redemption. It is certainly that, but it is also much more. Both the Old and New Testaments reveal to us a God who is both the creator and the sustainer of all things. It would be odd, therefore, if God's supreme act of redemption were limited to a narrow sliver of his creation—human souls. But that is precisely what many modern Christians think, and that explains why we struggle to connect the cross with the kingdom of heaven. The Gospel writers, who were not shaped by an individualistic culture, saw the cross as the hinge upon which all of history and creation turned. It wasn't simply "how Jesus saved *me*," but how his kingdom came to triumph over the whole world.

Gustaf Aulen articulated this more expansive vision of the cross this way: "The work of Christ is first and foremost a victory over the Powers which hold mankind in bondage: sin, death, and the devil. . . . The victory of Christ creates a new situation, bringing their rule to an end, and setting men free from their dominion."[2]

This view of the cross as defeating the "powers" that enslave both the world and humanity is known by theologians as *Christus Victor*, Latin for "Christ is victorious," and it helps explain why the Gospels devote so much attention to Jesus's death. For Matthew, Mark, Luke, and John, the cross is where the illegitimate rulers and kingdoms of the world were exposed, disarmed, and dethroned, and where the true King triumphed. For them, the cross is how the kingdom of heaven overthrew the kingdoms of the world.

 **READ MORE: Colossians 2:13–15; Luke 4:16–21**

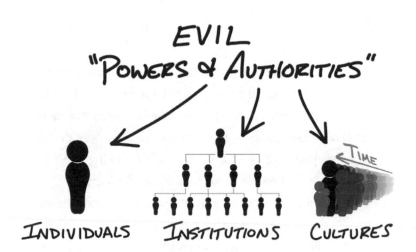

EVIL
"POWERS & AUTHORITIES"

INDIVIDUALS    INSTITUTIONS    CULTURES

**㉛ IF JESUS WAS SERIOUS . . .
THEN HIS KINGDOM HAS
DEFEATED BOTH PERSONAL
AND SYSTEMIC EVIL**

*CHRISTUS VICTOR IS A MORE COSMIC,* even apocalyptic,
vision of the cross than most of us are used to, but one that the
New Testament repeatedly affirms. To view the cross as the moment when the enemies of God's kingdom were defeated, we must

understand how the Bible defines these hostile "powers and authorities" (Col. 2:15).

Depending on your church tradition, you might assume that "powers and authorities" is a fancy way of talking about demonic forces. That is certainly a theme in the Gospels where Jesus metaphorically compares Satan to a strongman who has been tied up and his house plundered with the arrival of God's kingdom.

The apostle Paul, however, broadens our understanding of the "powers and authorities" to include much more than devils and demons. He recognizes that forces aligned against the kingdom of heaven permeate the systems and structures of society. They are the deeply formative ideas and patterns of behavior that we rarely recognize but which shape the way we think, act, and feel. I like Rich Villodas's definition: "Powers and authorities are spiritual forces that become hostile, taking root in individuals, ideologies, and institutions, with the goal of deception, division, and depersonalization."[1]

The New Testament sees God's enemies as more than personal demonic minions. The "powers and authorities" are also the systems of the world that conspire to accomplish the destructive intentions of those opposed to God's will. This explains why theologians see sin as inhabiting systems and not merely individuals. That includes governments, economic structures, corporations, media outlets, and cultural or social institutions that may have been established for human flourishing but that have been corrupted and co-opted by evil. When this happens, they become agents of deception, dehumanization, division, and ultimately death.

Consider the apartheid regime that dominated South Africa for most of the twentieth century. Certainly, individual South Africans were guilty of racial injustice, but over generations these evils became embedded in the country's culture, institutions, and structures so that even when individuals acted justly, the powers and authorities in South Africa continued to sinfully favor whites more than other citizens.

Bishop Desmond Tutu, who helped lead the South African resistance to apartheid, gave a sermon in the 1970s that articulated both the reality of evil powers at work in the systems of the world and our perspective as Christians who have overcome those powers through the cross. He said:

I am a bishop in the Church of God, I am 51 years old, yet I don't have a vote; an 18-year old, through a wonder of biological irrelevance—white skin—is able to vote. . . . They can remove Desmond Tutu. They can end the South African Council of Churches. But the Church of God goes on. The government must know that the Church is not frightened of any earthly power. . . . More are for us than can ever be against us. A vast throng no one could ever count, from every nation and every tribe, standing before the throne and before the Lamb, robed in white and bearing palms in their hands, shout together, 'Victory to our God!' We join with angels and archangels and the whole company of heaven."[2]

Why is the multiethnic church able to celebrate the victory of God over every enemy—including the systemic injustice of apartheid? Because Jesus has defeated the powers and authorities that stand against the kingdom of heaven. Tutu's sermon draws from the apostle John's vision where he saw a Lamb standing before the throne "looking as if it had been slain" (Rev. 5:6). The cross is where the powers and authorities of the world thought they had defeated Jesus. In fact, it was where Jesus and his kingdom defeated them.

 **READ MORE: Revelation 5:6–14; Colossians 2:13–15**

## 32 IF JESUS WAS SERIOUS . . . THEN HIS FOLLOWERS WILL BRING HEAVEN TO EARTH LIKE HE DID

**DURING HIS FAREWELL DISCOURSE** with his apostles, Jesus made one of the more shocking—and often misunderstood—promises found anywhere in the Gospels. He said, "Truly, truly, I say to you, whoever believes in me will also do the works that I do; and greater works than these will he do, because I am going to the Father" (John 14:12 ESV). This verse provokes an obvious and important question: What are the "greater works" Jesus's followers will do?

We've already looked at our culture's fixation on all things spectacular and the way it causes us to mistakenly focus on Jesus's power rather than on Jesus himself. Our cultural bias has also warped the way many have interpreted this verse. For those shaped by pop consumer Christianity, "greater works" is automatically assumed to mean more spectacular works. This view believes that because Jesus walked on water, healed the sick, and calmed storms, then to do greater works means the true disciples of Jesus will accomplish *even more astonishing* signs and wonders. In a culture drawn to the spectacular and in church traditions dedicated to attracting crowds, it's obvious why this interpretation is appealing.

However, there are a few problems with understanding "greater works" to mean *more astonishing* works. First, obviously most of those who follow Jesus are *not* doing more spectacular works than he performed. It's hard to do something more spectacular than raising the dead, which Jesus did on multiple occasions, and the last time I checked most Christians were not emptying the cemeteries. Therefore, this interpretation would immediately call into question the authenticity of the faith of nearly every Christian past and present.

Second, throughout the history of the church, most have not understood this verse to mean we would do more spectacular miracles than Jesus. This is a rather recent interpretation that gained traction with the arrival of more charismatic movements—particularly in the United States and in the Global South—in the twentieth century.

Throughout most of history, Christians have interpreted Jesus to mean his followers would do *more* works. In this case, "greater" means greater in quantity, scale, and influence. Remember, Jesus's public ministry was amazingly brief—approximately three years—and it was confined to a geographic area about the size of New Jersey. Before they died, the apostles Jesus was speaking to in John 14 would proclaim the gospel and make disciples from the Iberian Peninsula in the West to the Indian subcontinent in the East. Even in the book of Acts, we see more people put their faith in Christ through the ministry of the apostles than ever responded to the preaching of Jesus himself. In this regard, their works *were* greater than Jesus's.

Later generations of believers would go on to invent hospitals, educate countless millions, and mobilize efforts to feed, clothe, and comfort more people than any movement in history. Today alone the followers of Jesus will touch more lives than Jesus touched during his entire earthly ministry. We lose sight of this remarkable fact when we focus only on the method of our works rather than on their outcome. We assume that for works to be "greater" than Jesus's, they must be accomplished through some supernatural agency rather than human ingenuity. This is, of course, ridiculous.

Just as Jesus reunited heaven and earth through his presence, his words, and his actions, his followers now do the same thing. Sometimes the presence of the kingdom of heaven on earth is spectacular, but often it is subtle. In the end, what matters is that we feed a hungry child—*not* whether the food appeared miraculously or arrived on the back of a truck.

Maybe we need to rethink what qualifies as a miracle to begin with. After all, which is the greater wonder—Christ's power to transform water into wine, or his power to transform hearts to be generous, merciful, and loving? We should remember that God desires to manifest his kingdom *in* us, not merely through us.

 **READ MORE: John 14:6–14; Matthew 7:15–23**

HOW THE KINGDOM GREW THROUGH JESUS

HOW THE KINGDOM GROWS NOW

## 33 IF JESUS WAS SERIOUS . . . THEN THE KINGDOM OF HEAVEN IS EXPANDING BECAUSE HE IS WITH THE FATHER

**AS WE DISCUSSED** in the previous chapter, when Jesus told his disciples, "Truly, truly, I say to you, whoever believes in me will also do the works that I do; and greater works than these will he do, because I am going to the Father" (John 14:12), he did not mean that they would do more spectacular miracles. Rather, he meant that they would do more numerous and transformative kingdom acts. There is, however, another faithful way to understand Jesus's statement that has nothing to do with either the quantity or quality of the works but rather their *locality*.

It's helpful to look at another time Jesus spoke about something being "greater." In Matthew's Gospel, Jesus said, "Among those born of women there has not arisen anyone greater than John the Baptist; yet whoever is least in the kingdom of heaven is greater than he" (Matt. 11:11). Here Jesus is affirming John's greatness, but John's ministry occurred *before* Jesus announced the arrival of the kingdom—the great climax of history when God would reunite heaven and earth and restore all things. In this case, Jesus defines "greatness" based on one's location in history. To be the least significant person within the age of God's heavenly kingdom is greater than being the most significant person before it.

We apply this same logic of temporal location all the time in other areas—like athletics. Making a three-point shot in a basketball game is good. Hitting a three-pointer at the buzzer to win the championship is even greater. In this example, the actions are the same, but what makes one act greater is *when* it happens. Its greatness is determined by its moment in time rather than by the nature of the action. No one replays the video of a three-pointer sunk during practice, but the game-winning shot from half-court will be celebrated repeatedly. Likewise, Jesus affirms the greatness of John's life, but living within the kingdom of heaven on earth is, by virtue of its location in history, even greater.

Jesus may have been using similar logic in the Farewell Discourse when he spoke about his followers doing great works "because I am going to the Father." He links the greatness of their works with his relocation to be with the Father. Remember, the theme of the discourse so far has been Jesus leaving his disciples to return to the Father via the cross, resurrection, and ascension. The cross is how Jesus will be enthroned with God and begin his reign over all things. Therefore, his disciples' works will happen during this final age of the world, the great climax that all of history has been moving toward when heaven and earth are one.

While Jesus certainly did great works during his time on earth, after returning to the Father he is, in one sense, no longer on the court. Instead, he has taken up his rightful place coaching (i.e., ruling) while his followers play in the final championship. In this way, their actions on the court will exceed his in greatness because they will occur during his reign over heaven and earth, even as his authority as the true King of kings far exceeds theirs as his servants.

**READ MORE: John 14:6–14; Matthew 11:7–15**

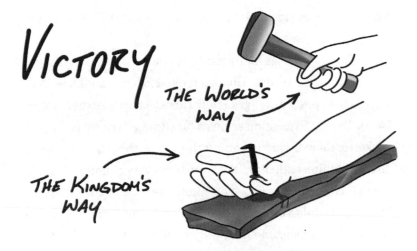

VICTORY

THE WORLD'S WAY →

→ THE KINGDOM'S WAY

## (34) IF JESUS WAS SERIOUS . . . THEN THE WAY OF GOD'S KINGDOM WILL ALWAYS BE THE WAY OF THE CROSS

**ON THE NIGHT OF HIS ARREST,** in his final conversation with his disciples, Jesus spoke to them about returning to his Father, preparing a place for them, and returning to take them to be with him. He was speaking of his death, resurrection, and second coming. Then Jesus added, "You know the way to the place where I am going" (John 14:4).

This verse confuses many readers, just as it confused his disciples at the time. In fact, Thomas replied to him, "Lord, we don't know where you are going, so how can we know the way?" (John 14:5). Thomas's question seems a bit strange because Jesus had spoken to them frequently about the cross—some scholars see a direct or indirect allusion to the cross in every chapter of John's Gospel. When Jesus said, "you know the way," he was saying, *I've already told you how I will return to the Father. Through humiliation, shame, and death. By surrendering everything and entrusting myself to the Father, I will also be glorified. This is the way.*

Like the first disciples, many Christians today are reluctant to accept this path. The worldly temptation for power, comfort, and success is so strong that we are drawn to Christian leaders and messages that say God wants us to grasp at these things. We seem chronically tempted to pursue the kingdom of heaven by employing the values of the world.

After Jesus was arrested and brought before Pilate, the Roman governor, he said, "My kingdom is not of this world. If it were, my servants would fight to prevent my arrest by the Jewish leaders. But now my kingdom is from another place" (John 18:36). Jesus was declaring that his kingdom, and those who belong to it, do not operate like the kingdoms of the world. The way of heaven is not coercion, violence, greed, or fear, and its citizens do not seek self-preservation or power above all else.

The temptation to divorce the work of Christ from the way of Christ, or to abandon the values of heaven for the values of earth, has done great harm throughout the history of the church. This temptation gains strength whenever we separate the *scope* of God's mission from the *nature* of God's mission.

Remember, he is in the process of redeeming "all things," and he is employing us in that work. A disciple of Jesus should be awestruck and even appropriately overwhelmed by the scale of this calling. Unfortunately, the world-changing scope of God's mission causes some to think accomplishing it will necessitate using the world's methods and values. After all, world changing is what empires, armies, and corporations do. Maybe the church should copy their strategies too.

This imperial approach is a terrible error that has led Christians into darkness and evil throughout history, and it continues to inflict great harm on congregations and communities today. Jamin Goggin and Kyle Strobel, in their book *The Way of the Dragon or the Way of the Lamb*, remind us that we can only pursue the mission of heaven using the methods of heaven, which always look like the humble self-sacrifice of Jesus. They write, "We are called as his people to participate in Christ's triumph over these powers by submitting to the way of the cross. We are called to be a cruciform people—to live according to the cross-shaped way of

Jesus. We are called to receive power in weakness, not power in our strength or in ourselves."[1]

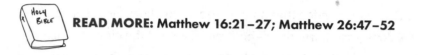 **READ MORE:** Matthew 16:21–27; Matthew 26:47–52

# PART 5

# THE KINGDOM OF THE WORLD HAS BECOME THE KINGDOM OF OUR LORD

## ACTS 1:6–11

Then they gathered around him and asked him, "Lord, are you at this time going to restore the kingdom to Israel?"

He said to them: "It is not for you to know the times or dates the Father has set by his own authority. But you will receive power when the Holy Spirit comes on you; and you will be my witnesses in Jerusalem, and in all Judea and Samaria, and to the ends of the earth."

After he said this, he was taken up before their very eyes, and a cloud hid him from their sight.

They were looking intently up into the sky as he was going, when suddenly two men dressed in white stood beside them. "Men of Galilee," they said, "why do you stand here looking into the sky? This same Jesus, who has been taken from you into heaven, will come back in the same way you have seen him go into heaven."

## 35   IF JESUS WAS SERIOUS . . . THEN GOD WILL RULE FOREVER WITH HIS PEOPLE ON EARTH, NOT IN HEAVEN

**AFTER HIS RESURRECTION,** Jesus continued to appear to his disciples and teach them for a period of forty days. We are told in the opening chapter of Acts that he spoke to them about the kingdom of God, and the disciples asked when the kingdom would be fully revealed. They wanted to know when heaven and earth would be reunited, and God's rule established for all to see. Jesus did not answer the question but instead promised them power to be his witnesses throughout the world. Then, after commanding them to wait in Jerusalem for the arrival of the Holy Spirit, Jesus ascended into the sky—more literally, the heavens (Acts 1:10).

Two angels then appeared and said to them, "Why do you stand here looking into the sky? This same Jesus, who has been taken from you into heaven, will come back in the same way you have seen him go into heaven" (Acts 1:11). Remember, ancient cultures used the same word to mean the sky, the heavens, and God's spiritual realm. Therefore, when Jesus was "taken up before their very eyes" (Acts 1:9) and disappeared, the disciples understood that he was returning to God's presence. The message of the angels to the disciples was not, *someday you will also leave the earth and join Jesus in the heavens*, but rather, *Jesus will someday return from the heavens and be with you again on the earth.*

The angels' words are important because they indicate where Jesus's followers should focus their hope. Our goal should not be to follow Jesus into the heavens but to anticipate him returning to reign upon the earth. Unfortunately, this is not the orientation of popular Christianity with its heaven-centric mental map. Today, even when Christians do speak of Jesus's return, it is often framed as a rescue mission in which Jesus will appear descending from the clouds to gather his people and take them to heaven before the earth is destroyed. But that idea is never mentioned by the angels, and its popularity reveals how our heaven-centric mental map has warped other doctrines of our faith, including Jesus's ascension and promised return.

What the angels spoke of in Acts 1 is depicted later in Revelation 21 with vivid and symbolic imagery. There, John records a vision of God's throne coming down out of the heavens to the earth and a loud voice declaring, "Look! God's dwelling place is now among the people, and he will dwell with them. They will be his people" (Rev. 21:2–3). This is the restoration of the kingdom the disciples had asked Jesus about. This is the reunification of heaven and earth. Notice that rather than God's people ascending into the heavens to be with him, God descends from the heavens to be with his people on earth, exactly as the angels promised.

This climax of the biblical story does not show Jesus ruling the cosmos from heaven. Instead, his throne is established upon a renewed and redeemed earth. Likewise, Christ's people are not whisked away to dwell in his presence in heaven. Instead, heaven descends to earth so that Jesus may be with us. Rather than a heaven-centric vision of the future, what the New Testament describes is a Jesus-centric vision of the future *here on earth*.

 **READ MORE: Matthew 6:9–10; Revelation 21:1–4**

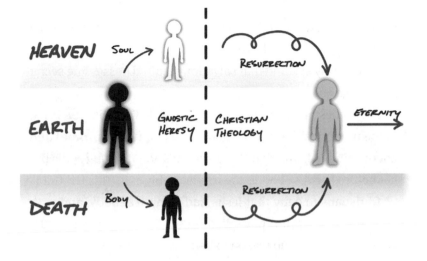

## 36  IF JESUS WAS SERIOUS . . . THEN GOD IS REDEEMING OUR BODIES, NOT JUST OUR SOULS

**THE HEAVEN-CENTRIC MENTAL MAP** carried by many people says heaven is a celestial paradise inhabited by disembodied souls. This view assumes that our bodies are temporary and will return to the dust, while our souls are eternal and will endure for eternity. Such elevation of the spiritual and disregard for the material is similar to an ancient heresy called Gnosticism. Its name comes from the Greek word *gnosis*, meaning "knowledge," and it's rooted in a Greek philosophical tradition that believed all physical matter was inherently evil and that salvation required possessing secret knowledge about God.

When these ideas intersected with early Christianity, it led to the unbiblical belief that God cared about the spiritual and not the physical, and that the gospel was about saving souls but not bodies because bodies are irredeemably evil. This led Gnostic Christians to deny that Jesus had a physical body, and with no body he could not have died on the cross. Of course, if he never died, there's no reason to believe in his physical resurrection. From top to bottom, Gnosticism was a denial of the gospel. Most scholars agree that John was targeting this heresy when he wrote that every spirit that does not acknowledge that Jesus Christ has come in the flesh "is the spirit of the antichrist" (1 John 4:2–3).

Today, in different forms, Gnostic-like beliefs remain dangerously common among Christians. Many Christians still assume God cares only about souls and spirits, and that the goal of salvation through Christ must be to escape from our bodies to occupy a non-physical heaven. Within evangelical communities, Gnosticism's condemnation of bodies has been subtly at work behind "purity culture," which warns of the dangers of sexuality and the evil of physical desires. Taken together, this focus on "saving souls" and avoiding the "temptations of the flesh" has made pop Christianity into a kind of neo-Gnosticism that celebrates the spiritual and condemns the physical.

But this understanding contradicts everything we know about Jesus's ministry and his miracles. If he was concerned only with saving souls, why did Jesus spend so much time healing bodies? And if physical matter isn't part of God's redemptive plan, why does the New Testament aggressively and repeatedly emphasize the *physical* resurrection of Jesus?

In 1 Corinthians 15, Paul argues that Jesus's resurrection is the "first fruits" or the prototype for the rest of God's salvation. Paul says that our bodies, like Jesus's, will also be raised, transformed, and glorified when Christ returns. The physical creation itself will share in this glory and be set free from its captivity to death and decay (Rom. 8:20–21). In other words, the physical reality of Jesus's resurrection is why we believe in our physical salvation and the physical salvation of the world. Put simply, the bodily resurrection of Jesus means matter matters.

This has huge implications for our lives and callings as Christians. It means we must reject both the overt and subtle forms of Gnosticism that still infect our faith—like the tendency to celebrate vocations that care for souls and focus on heaven while dismissing vocations that care for bodies and the earth. We must also uproot the assumptions in many Christian communities that God cares about the next world but has given up on this one, or that a spiritually mature Christian must transcend their body and its weaknesses to occupy a realm of ideas, theology, and knowledge alone. The physical resurrection of Jesus reveals that God cares about every part of his creation—both the material and the spiritual—and he is in the process of redeeming all of it.

 **READ MORE: 1 Corinthians 15:20–49**

SAME BODY
RAISED &
TRANSFORMED

SAME EARTH
RAISED &
TRANSFORMED

## 37 IF JESUS WAS SERIOUS . . . THEN HIS RESURRECTED BODY IS A PREVIEW OF THE RESURRECTED EARTH

**THE WIDELY HELD BELIEF** that God is concerned with redeeming souls but not bodies is utterly unbiblical. This common assumption is shown to be mistaken through Jesus's miracles of healing and especially his physical, bodily resurrection. There is another, similar error that dominates much of modern Christianity—the widely held belief that God will completely destroy the earth and replace it with a new one. Christians often cite this view as a reason to downplay both environmental concerns and social injustices. If everything on earth is going to be destroyed anyway, they argue, wouldn't working to alleviate physical suffering or avoid climate catastrophe be like rearranging the deck chairs on the *Titanic*?

This belief in the utter destruction of the world in favor of a spiritual salvation in heaven is what led Oliver Wendell Holmes to declare, "Some people are so heavenly minded that they are no earthly good."[1] His statement is rooted in a vision of the future where heaven and earth remain separate realms, and where the spiritual (heaven) is valued while the material (earth) is not. Yet no one could ever say that Jesus was only heavenly minded. He devoted his ministry to healing bodies, feeding the hungry, liberating the oppressed, and mending social divisions (see Luke 4:16–21). The fact that Holmes's statement does apply to so many Christians today reveals we've gotten something very wrong. A closer examination of Jesus's resurrection can help us diagnose our error and correct it.

The New Testament repeatedly identifies Jesus's resurrection as both the beginning and the pattern for God's re-creation of all things. First, Paul says, our future, resurrected bodies will be just like Jesus's resurrected body (1 Cor. 15:42–49). Second, this resurrection power will also be unleashed throughout creation, which will share the same glory that awaits our transformed bodies

(Rom. 8:19–21). Therefore, if we want to understand what future awaits us and the earth, we must look to Jesus's resurrection as the prototype.

While many Christians assume this world will be completely destroyed and replaced at the end of history, that is *not* the pattern established by Jesus's resurrection. On Easter, we celebrate that the tomb was *empty*. While Jesus's body was certainly transformed and glorified when resurrected, it was not replaced. He was not given a new body with his old one left in the grave. On this point, the Gospel writers and apostles are unwavering. The same body that was crucified on Friday was raised back to life on Sunday. If Jesus's body had been left to rot in the tomb and replaced with a new one, Christians would not celebrate Jesus's *resurrection* but rather his *reincarnation*.

Even worse, we could not say the enemy has been defeated because death would still receive a consolation prize—the tortured corpse of a Nazarene carpenter. To prove this fact, Jesus showed his disciples the wounds from his crucifixion. His body was raised and transformed, but it was still the *same body*. That is a crucial point with massive implications for our faith and how we think about the future of heaven and earth.

Just as Jesus's resurrection exhibits both discontinuity (his body was changed) and continuity (it was the same body), so our future bodies and the future creation will be marked by dramatic trans-formation *and* remarkable sameness. The New Testament reveals

God's intent to redeem this world (continuity) but also transform and glorify it by reuniting it with heaven (discontinuity). The earth will be made new and yet it will be the *same earth.*

That means the earth you and I occupy today will be the same earth we will occupy for eternity. It will be an earth set free from death, disease, and decay. We will recognize this planet in the age to come, just as Jesus's disciples recognized him and his scars after the resurrection, and yet the world will also be changed as the curtain between heaven and earth is removed forever.

 **READ MORE: Romans 8:18–25; Luke 24:36–43**

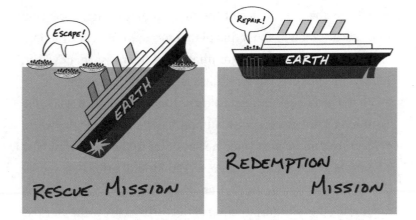

### 38   IF JESUS WAS SERIOUS . . . THEN THE WORLD WILL NOT BE REPLACED BUT RENEWED

**SOME CHRISTIANS, UPON HEARING** that the New Testament does *not* teach that we will spend eternity in heaven but that the renewed earth will be our permanent home, will immediately counter with 2 Peter 3. There, the apostle says the earth will be "destroyed" by fire and that "we are looking forward to a new heaven and a new earth" (2 Pet. 3:10–13). These verses are often cited to justify the notion that "this world is not my home" and to dismiss the importance of the present earth. After all, if God doesn't care enough about this planet to save it from destruction, why should we? A closer examination of the passage, however, reveals this popular interpretation is precisely backward.

First, Peter begins by reminding us that in the days of Noah, the Lord judged the wicked with a flood that "destroyed" the world (2 Pet. 3:6). In the next verse he says that in the same way, "the present heavens and earth are reserved for fire, being kept for the day of judgment and destruction of the ungodly" (v. 7). Peter is comparing the *future* destruction of the earth by fire to the *previous* destruction of the earth by water. But the flood story in Genesis does *not* say the earth was literally destroyed and replaced with a new planet, so this cannot be what Peter has in mind. Instead, just as the floodwaters cleansed the earth and washed away all unrighteousness, Peter means the wicked people, institutions, and systems that perpetuate evil will one day be destroyed by fire. Like the "destruction" caused by the flood, the destruction of the world by fire will be a cleansing of unrighteousness and a renewing of the earth.

A few verses later, Peter adds that "the heavens will disappear with a roar; the elements will be destroyed by fire" (3:10). Some say this must refer to the utter destruction of the earth, with only the souls of those saved by God being rescued from the flames. Again, a closer look merits a different interpretation. These

174

"elements," Peter says, will be "destroyed by fire." This can't refer to the destruction of the earth because his next words are, "and the earth and the works that are done on it will be *exposed*." The Greek word for "elements" here is often translated as "heavenly bodies," meaning the sun, moon, and stars that are associated with the heavens throughout Scripture. According to Peter, the heavens will be pulled back to *expose* or *reveal* the earth.

Peter was employing common imagery from his culture, which viewed the heavens, or the atmosphere, like a garment or blanket covering the earth. Removing the heavens leaves the earth naked and unable to hide from God and his judgment. We find this model of the cosmos represented in the architecture of the Jewish temple. According to the Old Testament's description of the temple, thick blue curtains embroidered with angels representing the sky ("the heavens") separated the main room in the temple—the Holy Place decorated with trees, flowers, and fruit to represent the earth—from the inner room—the Holy of Holies entirely covered in gold to represent God's throne. Therefore, rolling up the temple curtains—removing the heavens—would fully expose the earth to God's presence.

Once we understand this imagery and Peter's comparison to Noah's flood, the apostle's point becomes clear. He's not saying the earth will be materially destroyed and replaced but that the earth—and all of the evil upon it—will no longer be *hidden*. It will be revealed and purged away by the fire of God. This is language common in both the Old and New Testaments and refers to the refinement of metal. Paul said the day of judgment will be a fire that reveals the quality of each person's work (1 Cor. 3:13), and in another letter Peter said that trials reveal the purity of our faith the way a refiner's fire purifies gold (1 Pet. 1:7). In all these texts fire reveals, purifies, and purges.

One final detail. In Greek, there are two words meaning "new." *Neos* emphasizes chronological newness, meaning new in age or time. *Kainos* emphasizes qualitative newness, meaning new in condition or quality. When the apostles speak of a "new heaven" and "new earth," as Peter does in this chapter, they use the word *kainos*. The New Testament does not teach that the earth will be replaced but that it will be made like new in quality by the exposure and destruction of all evil. As in the days of the flood, everything and everyone that is opposed to God's kingdom will be revealed and purged away—but this time by the consuming fire of God's presence. What will emerge is a transformed and glorified earth.

**READ MORE: 2 Peter 3:8–12; Matthew 24:36–51**

HEAVEN       HEAVEN

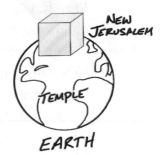

EARTH       EARTH

## ㊴ IF JESUS WAS SERIOUS . . . THEN THE NEW JERUSALEM REPRESENTS THE REUNION OF HEAVEN AND EARTH

**REVELATION IS A NOTORIOUSLY DIFFICULT** book to inter-
pret. It is an ancient literary genre totally foreign to the modern
world, and it is loaded with apocalyptic symbolism, convoluted
timelines, and cultural references we easily miss. Consider the way

John describes the heavenly city, New Jerusalem, which descends to the earth. He says the massive metropolis is "pure gold" and with the dimensions of a perfect cube—equal in length, width, and height.

If taken literally, John's vision faces considerable problems. For example, how exactly do people inhabit a city 1,400 miles tall, given the earth's atmosphere is only 50 miles high and only a fraction of it is able to sustain life? The New Jerusalem in John's vision is clearly symbolic, but what does it represent? Few in our culture would immediately understand John's vision, but his original audience would have grasped the meaning of the golden cube city immediately.

The New Jerusalem represents the Holy of Holies, the innermost sanctuary of the temple in Jerusalem where the Israelites believed God's presence resided. The Holy of Holies was the Lord's throne room. This inner sanctum was cube shaped; the floor, walls, and ceiling all had the same dimensions. Every surface and object in the Holy of Holies was covered with gold. The room was inaccessible to anyone apart from the high priest, who was permitted entrance once a year.

Therefore, with his vision of a gold, cube-shaped city descending from the heavens to earth, John is saying that in the age to come the Holy of Holies, the very presence of God, will fill the earth, and access to God will be unhindered and unending. All of Christ's people will dwell with him in the Holy of Holies, and there will be no separation between heaven and earth. The apostle wants to fill us with hope for the day when God will again dwell with his people on earth, just as he walked with the man and woman in Eden in the beginning.

 **READ MORE: Revelation 21:1–4; 1 Kings 6:19–28**

**A.**

KINGDOM
OF HEAVEN

KINGDOM
OF EVIL

**B.**

KINGDOM
OF HEAVEN

KINGDOM
OF EVIL

**C.**

KINGDOM
OF HEAVEN

KINGDOM
OF EVIL

How Do You
Imagine
Eternity?

**D.**

"THE KINGDOM OF THE
WORLD HAS BECOME
THE KINGDOM OF OUR
LORD!" REV.11:15

**40** **IF JESUS WAS SERIOUS . . .
THEN IN THE AGE TO COME
THERE WILL BE ONE KINGDOM,
NOT TWO**

**WHEN WE REACH THE FINAL CHAPTERS** of the Bible, we discover imagery that echoes back to the opening chapters of Genesis. This is deliberate and cements the link between the Hebrew vision of creation and the Christian vision of redemption in which God is restoring the unity of heaven and earth first encountered in the garden where the Lord and his people lived together.

The opening words of the creation narrative speak of darkness over the face of the deep: "The Spirit of God was hovering over the waters" (Gen. 1:2). From this dark, primordial sea the Lord brings forth light, land, and life. In many ancient civilizations, including ancient Israel, the sea was a symbol of chaos and disorder. It was a mysterious and ominous realm often associated with evil and forces opposed to the God of life and light. From the opening pages of the Bible, however, we discover the Lord's power over the sea. He subdues the forces of chaos and creates order, harmony, and abundance.

We see this again in the flood story when the Lord breaks the boundaries of the sea and water destroys the earth, but he protects one family from the deluge and renews creation. We also see the Lord's deliverance of his people from Egypt through the sea while the waters then destroy Pharaoh and his army. We even find this theme repeated in the famous story of Jesus calming the storm on the Sea of Galilee. "Who is this?" his apostles marvel. "Even the wind and the waves obey him!" (Mark 4:41). The answer, of course, is that Jesus is the same King over creation who spoke over the waters in the beginning to draw order from chaos.

All of this helps us make sense of Revelation 21, where the apostle John includes a strange detail about his vision of the redeemed earth. He says, "There was no longer any sea" (Rev. 21:1). Does this mean in the future we will occupy a world without oceans? Reading John's vision literally is both practically and biblically shortsighted. Practically, we know a world without seas is uninhabitable because oceans are necessary to sustain the atmosphere, weather, and terrestrial life. Biblically, John's vision must be read in the larger context of the Bible in which the sea represents evil and chaos. The apostle is not making a *scientific* observation about the age to come, but a *theological* one.

Many Christians envision eternity as divided territory between those aligned with God occupying his heavenly kingdom and his enemies forever banished to a miserable place outside of it. But John communicates a more decisive victory. By announcing the elimination of the sea, John is saying that when God's redemption of all things is complete, the forces of evil, chaos, and death represented by the sea throughout the Scriptures will not merely be contained—they will be *abolished*: "There will be no more death or mourning or crying or pain, for the old order of things has passed away" (Rev. 21:4).

Rather than a divided new creation partly occupied by God's kingdom and partly by the defeated forces of evil, John offers a vision of the future where God's perfect rule extends over all things. On this point the Bible is consistent and clear—in the age to come there will only be one kingdom, not two. We will celebrate with all the hosts of heaven how "the kingdom of the world has become the kingdom of our Lord and of his Messiah" (Rev. 11:15).

 **READ MORE: Revelation 21:1–4; Mark 4:35–41**

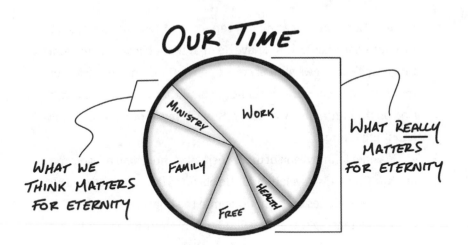

**41** # IF JESUS WAS SERIOUS . . .
# THEN OUR WORK NOW
# MATTERS FOR ETERNITY

**WHAT WE BELIEVE ABOUT THE FUTURE** determines what we
believe matters in the present. This is why a heaven-centric view of
the Christian life is so damaging. It severely limits what we believe
Jesus cares about and, therefore, narrows the mission and works
his followers engage in. For example, if eternity will be in a heaven
occupied by souls and everything else will burn, then what is the

point of Christians creating art, repairing unjust institutions, or inventing vaccines? Sadly, I have heard Christian leaders proclaim precisely these views with absolute conviction. Once we discover that heaven is *not* our eternal home, and that we will reign with God on the earth, then we must rethink many of our assumptions about the future.

Consider John's vision of the redeemed world where heaven and earth are united in Revelation 21. He observes the rulers of the earth bringing the glories of the nations into the holy city (Rev. 21:24). John is referencing something first written centuries earlier by the Hebrew prophet Isaiah (Isa. 60:1–7). Richard Mouw explains the meaning of both John's vision and Isaiah's prophecy. Rather than destroying the artifacts and creations of pagan cultures, Mouw says, God will instead transform and redeem them for his glory:

When the kings come marching in, then, they bring the best of their nations—even the cultural goods that had been deployed against God and his people. The final vision of the City is one filled, not just with God's glory and presence, not just with his own stunningly beautiful architectural designs, not just with redeemed persons from every cultural background—but with redeemed human culture too.[1]

This vision of eternity being filled with the art, literature, technology, music, and other artifacts created throughout human history is completely absent from most Christians' understanding of the future. Yet the Bible presents a vision of a terrestrial, embodied eternity that looks very much like human civilization does now but without evil, injustice, death, or disease.

The biblical vision carries two important implications. First, it means any vision of eternity as a never-ending worship service is completely wrong. In the age to come, there will still be entertainment, commerce, technology, and discovery. When heaven and earth are one, we will still create art, music, and literature. Human cultures with all their activities will continue, will grow, and will flourish to the glory of God. It will be the world God always intended from the beginning—a world where we fill the earth and create cultures in partnership with God and as his representatives (Gen. 1:26–28).

Second, if the things we do and create now—the glories of the nations—will be welcomed into the kingdom of heaven on earth, then the work we do now truly matters for eternity, and not just the work we label "ministry." Imagine how different our world would be if more Christians believed this. What wrongs ignored by the church would be engaged and made right? What glimpses of God's beauty would be revealed through the skills of artists filled with his Spirit? What evidence would we see of God's will being done on earth as it is in heaven?

 **READ MORE: Revelation 21:22–27; Isaiah 60:1–7**

# NOTES

**Chapter 1 ... Then Our View of Heaven Must Match His**

1. Dallas Willard, *Divine Conspiracy: Rediscovering Our Hidden Life in God* (San Francisco: HarperSanFrancisco, 1998), 71.

**Chapter 2 ... Then We Should Focus on Heaven and Earth, Not Heaven and Hell**

1. Jon Collins and Tim Mackie, "Heaven and Earth Q+R," *BibleProject Podcast*, February 12, 2016, 44:31, https://bibleproject.com/podcast/heaven-earth-q-r.

**Chapter 3 ... Then He Is the Gateway between Heaven and Earth**

1. Hans Urs von Balthasar, *Prayer* (San Francisco: Ignatius, 1986), 52.

**Chapter 6 ... Then the Kingdom of Heaven Restores All Things**

1. Unidentified pastor, quoted in Scot McKnight, *The King Jesus Gospel: The Original Good News Revisited* (Grand Rapids: Zondervan, 2016), 27.

2. McKnight, *King Jesus Gospel*, 130.

**Chapter 7 ... Then God Gives Us the Kingdom of Heaven Joyfully**

1. Frank Newport, "Most Americans Still Believe in God," Gallup, June 29, 2016, https://news.gallup.com/poll/193271/americans-believe-god.aspx.

2. Erin Duffin, "Church Attendance of Americans in 2021," *Statista*, September 30, 2022, https://www.statista.com/statistics/245491/church-attendance-of-americans.

**Chapter 9 ... Then Why Did He Teach So Mysteriously about the Kingdom of Heaven?**

1. Emily Dickinson, "Tell all the truth but tell it slant," in *The Poems of Emily Dickinson: Reading Edition* (Cambridge, MA: Belknap, 1998), available at https://www.poetryfoundation.org/poems/56824/tell-all-the-truth-but-tell-it-slant-1263.

2. Gary M. Burge, *Jesus, the Middle Eastern Storyteller* (Grand Rapids: Zondervan, 2009), 22.

### Chapter 10 . . . Then Why Do So Many People Reject the Kingdom of Heaven?

1. For more on the tendency of people to behave irrationally, I recommend Michael Lewis's book, *The Undoing Project: A Friendship That Changed Our Minds* (New York: Norton, 2017), about two psychologists who won the Nobel Prize for proving the human mind is hardwired to make irrational decisions.

2. C. S. Lewis, *The Weight of Glory* (New York: HarperCollins, 2001), 26.

### Chapter 11 . . . Then Joy, Not Misery, Should Mark Those Who Enter the Kingdom of Heaven

1. *Collins Dictionary*, s.v. "Sacrifice," https://www.collinsdictionary.com/us/dictionary/english/sacrifice.

### Chapter 14 . . . Then We Will Be Surprised by Who Enters the Kingdom of Heaven

1. John Newton, *The Amazing Works of John Newton* (United States: Bridge-Logos, 2009), 338.

### Chapter 16 . . . Then Evil Is a Real Problem That Will Be Overcome by the Kingdom of Heaven

1. Stephen Fry, "Stephen Fry on God | The Meaning of Life," YouTube video, 2:24, posted by RTÉ - Ireland's National Public Service Media on January 28, 2015, https://youtu.be/-suvkwNYSQo.

2. Russell Baker, *Growing Up* (New York: Congdon and Weed, 1982), 61.

3. Richard Dawkins, "God's Utility Function," *Scientific American*, November 1995, 85.

### Chapter 17 . . . Then We Should Not Confuse Heaven's Power with Human Power

1. Stephen J. Dubner, "How to Launch a Behavior-Change Revolution," *Freakonomics Radio*, episode 306, October 25, 2017, https://freakonomics.com/podcast/how-to-launch-a-behavior-change-revolution.

### Chapter 19 . . . Then Miracles Are Signs That the Kingdom of Heaven Is among Us

1. C. S. Lewis, *The Lion, the Witch and the Wardrobe* (United Kingdom: HarperCollins, 2005), 80.

### Chapter 20 . . . Then We Must Avoid Two Mistakes about Miracles

1. Thomas Schreiner, "Why I Am a Cessationist," The Gospel Coalition, January 22, 2014, https://www.thegospelcoalition.org/article/cessationist.

### Chapter 21 ... Then the Kingdom of Heaven Confronts Our Fear of Scarcity

1. Walter Brueggemann, *Deep Memory, Exuberant Hope: Contested Truth in a Post-Christian World* (Minneapolis: Fortress, 2000), 70.

2. Samuel Sommers, quoted in Heather McGhee, *The Sum of Us: What Racism Costs Everyone and How We Can Prosper Together* (New York: One World, 2021), 6.

3. McGhee, *Sum of Us*, 6.

### Chapter 22 ... Then Abundance Is about God's Kingdom, Not Our Consumer Desires

1. Ken Copeland, *The Laws of Prosperity* (Tulsa, OK: Harrison House, 2012), quoted in Tara Isabella Burton, "The Prosperity Gospel, Explained: Why Joel Osteen Believes That Prayer Can Make You Rich," *Vox*, September 1, 2017, https://www.vox.com/identities /2017/9/1/15951874/prosperity-gospel-explained-why-joel-osteen-believes-prayer -can-make-you-rich-trump.

2. David Van Biema and Jeff Chu, "Does God Want You to Be Rich?," *TIME*, September 10, 2006, https://content.time.com/time/magazine/article/0,9171,1533448,00 .html.

### Chapter 23 ... Then Life in the Kingdom of Heaven Doesn't Hurry

1. John Ortberg, *The Life You've Always Wanted: Spiritual Disciplines for Ordinary People* (Grand Rapids: Zondervan, 1997), 84.

2. Carl Jung, quoted in John Mark Comer, *The Ruthless Elimination of Hurry: How to Stay Emotionally Healthy and Spiritually Alive in the Chaos of the Modern World* (Colorado Springs: WaterBrook, 2019), 20.

3. Comer, *Ruthless Elimination of Hurry*, 20.

### Chapter 27 ... Then He's Not Building You a Mansion in Heaven

1. David Roach, "Heaven Tourism Books Pulled from Nearly 200 Christian Bookstores," *Christianity Today*, March 25, 2015, https://www.christianitytoday.com/news /2015/march/heaven-tourism-books-pulled-lifeway-90-minutes-in-heaven.html.

2. Jesus's Farewell Discourse is defined as either three chapters (John 14–16) or four chapters (John 14–17). Some do not include John 17 in the discourse because it is primarily a prayer Jesus expresses to the Father rather than a conversation with his disciples.

### Chapter 30 ... Then Heaven's Enemies Were Defeated through the Cross

1. James D. Miller, *Looking at the Cross*, Being Reformed: Faith Seeking Understanding (Louisville: Congregational Ministries Publishing, Presbyterian Church USA, 2012), 8–9.

2. Gustaf Aulen, *Christus Victor: An Historical Study of the Three Main Types of the Idea of Atonement*, trans. A. G. Herbert (London: SPCK, 1931), 20.

### Chapter 31 ... Then His Kingdom Has Defeated Both Personal and Systemic Evil

1. Rich Villodas, *Good and Beautiful and Kind: Becoming Whole in a Fractured World* (Colorado Springs: WaterBrook, 2022), 28.

2. Desmond Tutu, "The Church of God Goes On," *Living Church* 185, no. 16 (October 17, 1982): 6, quoted in Fleming Rutledge, *The Crucifixion: Understanding the Death of Jesus Christ* (Grand Rapids: Eerdmans, 2015), 383–84.

### Chapter 34 ... Then the Way of God's Kingdom Will Always Be the Way of the Cross

1. Jamin Goggin and Kyle Strobel, *The Way of the Dragon or the Way of the Lamb: Searching for Jesus' Path of Power in a Church That Has Abandoned It* (Nashville: Thomas Nelson, 2017), 78–79.

### Chapter 37 ... Then His Resurrected Body Is a Preview of the Resurrected Earth

1. This quote is widely attributed to Oliver Wendell Holmes, though no original source has been located.

### Chapter 41 ... Then Our Work Now Matters for Eternity

1. Richard Mouw, *When the Kings Come Marching In*, rev. ed. (Grand Rapids: Eerdmans, 2002), 20.